Nuggets from the Gold Mine

TABLE OF CONTENTS

Introduction

The book you hold in your hand has been carefully written, rewritten, prayed over, edited over and over, and finally years later I am satisfied and ready for publishing! "Nuggets" came to me because of the "nuggets of gold" the Lord revealed to me, and the Gold Mine is the Word of God.

It was while I was searching for the perfect lessons for my students at Charis Bible College (Then Colorado Bible College) that many of these revelations came to me. I owe Andrew Wommack a debt of gratitude for allowing me the privilege of teaching in his Bible College.

Because of Andrew's influence, our marriage was healed in the early to mid-1980's. Our Golden Wedding Anniversary (50 years) was celebrated in 2018. We owe the success of our marriage and our ministry to Andrew. It was through his meetings that we met most of our ministry friends we have today. We will complete 43 years of full-time and traveling ministry this year, 2020.

This book is also dedicated to my husband, Clifton, who is my biggest fan and treasured friend. My children cheer me on and are the greatest joys of my life.

Introduction

As this book is released in 2020, I have realized that this is our 50th year of serving the Lord and saving souls, teaching, ministering, from Indiana to Florida, back to Indiana to Colorado, and back to Indiana and finally here in Missouri! Our year of Jubilee! Our adventures have been worldwide and as deep as the ocean!

Word from the Author

This set of teachings is a collection of a few that are my personal favorites. Most of what I am sharing here came to me by "divine revelation", meaning I did not hear anyone else teach these truths, nor did I read them in books, just THE BOOK. Maybe a few were inspired by another minister or friend, and I do give credit where it is due. My first professionally published book, Your Rose Will Bloom Again (available on Amazon and in bookstores) has references to some of what is included here. I have gone into more detail in Nuggets, and a deeper study than Rose. These Nuggets are fresh, updated, and revised revelation, and I pray you receive encouragement and hope for the future from the words I have written here. Clifton also has an inspiring book, a transcribed message on SAINT OR SINNER? In my Grace Nugget, I am expounding on what I learned from his teaching. Smile.

I am including some updates on testimonies I shared in my Rose book, which is the story of my life's spiritual journey. I share these to encourage the reader! This is for YOU! What God has done for me, He will do for anyone.

God is the center of all I think and try to project. Looking through the lens of scripture has saved me from deep grief. I understand that we must all "work out our own salvation with fear and trembling", but we can learn from others and their mistakes, and we can be led to follow another's example. The Apostle Paul said to "follow me as I follow Christ." I have learned much from my matriarchs and patriarchs of the faith, both in my generation and from the men and women of the bible. My life has been impacted in a positive way. My prayer is that this book will be an inspiration and a help to you in your own journey with the Lord. The main thing I have learned since I first started writing this is that people need a revelation of God's love for *THEMSELVES PERSONALLY*. It is a "forever life changer", realizing the Love of God! We will talk about that as we go along.

In 2020 there is a fresh wind blowing across the country, and a "Great Awakening" among all flesh, both saved and unsaved! God is bringing all prophetic words from the past centuries into a perfect line up. Our part in the meantime is to draw close to God and listen to Him, then follow Him! As I have grown in the things of God, I have updated this book to be a light of grace and love and seeing ourselves the way God sees us.

God Bless, and Happy Reading!

Update on Cody
July 2018 – May 2020

In my first book, <u>Your Rose Will Bloom Again</u>, I told the story of Cody. How he was born when I was almost 40 years old, how God spoke to us that he would be a "singing evangelist" and be a restorer of our lives, and a helper in our old age. These prophetic words were given to us while I was still pregnant, and by others soon after he was born.

The fulfillment of this prophesy was a long time coming, and seemed impossible! His drug addiction, suicide attempts, and general state of being made things seem like it was never going to happen. We stood on the Word, and believed, "hope against hope." His drug addiction continued for 15 years.

Seven of those years were hard core needles, heroin and meth. I told some stories in <u>ROSE</u>, but will move on in this present narrative.

Cody was a fun little boy. He was smart and talented, and a blessed one, as he was able to travel with us in ministry, literally across the United States and all over the world. People loved him everywhere we went.

However, after some life altering circumstances in our

family, Clifton and I recovered and were able to handle the deep wounds we faced, but Cody did not know how to cope with the pain. At 15 years old he lost everything he owned in a fire, (clothes, video projects, expensive camera, all equipment he had for music and his "stuff") and we moved away from "home" to another state to follow our call to minister, which also caused him to have to leave all his friends. We moved from our home town in Indiana to Missouri.

He became a drug addict, and was on and off drugs for all those years, in and out of rehab, jail, five prisons, and finally hard-core prison, for breaking probation. I will not rehearse here the horrendous transgressions and the heartbreak we suffered, but you can read about it in "Rose".

While in County Jail Cody had an encounter with the Almighty Himself! From that point everything was different. The time spent in rehab was good, and Cody became a leader, and someone the recovering men looked to for help. He led many to the Lord in salvation, and helped all who came to him. Let me say also, though, that he was in rehab three times, relapsing. Don't give up on your kids or loved ones.

He was to be released in March 2017. I will not go into detail here, but his release was cancelled 6 days before he was to come home. It was a false allegation, a spiritual persecution. I can't describe the pain, the disappointment, and the grief we all endured.

I called the prison, I talked to 12 different ones who shifted me all over the prison, to no avail. I called the State Offices of DOC and spoke with the highest-ranking men and women there. I called and wrote to the Governor of Missouri. Nothing. Cody was placed in the "hole", solitary confinement, until his window of opportunity to file a grievance had passed. The guards refused him a pencil and paper.

I found some scripture, and I had my prayer team before the Lord, interceding for Cody. Believing he would be vindicated. No. It did not happen.

Now, I cannot pass up an opportunity to teach here!

When we find ourselves with "seemingly" unanswered prayer, we must do ONE THING – TRUST anyway! Trust God. Have faith in GOD. Do not look at the circumstances and wonder "why?", but rather, look to God and know He is on your side, always working in your behalf, and there is something you don't know that He knows. God is working things around for the good of everybody. We are not instructed to "understand", but to TRUST!

When the release was revoked, Cody was assigned to a hard core, steel bars, no counsellors, no case worker, no classes, just the 6x9 cell with metal doors and a slit.

No windows, no A/C, nothing!

The first time we visited him there – a three-hour drive from our home – I did not think I was going to make it through our visitation time allowance. The "light" was gone from Cody's eyes. He had had the wind sucked out of his sails, and we were all beyond devastated. I left there crying and told Clifton I did not think I could ever go back there. All our plans were gone. Cody was registered for Bible College in Colorado, I had found him a perfect place to stay, and we had been promised $2000 in college tuition plus he was offered a job making way above minimum wage. Now, here he was, stuck in this hell hole.

When we got back home that day, we were sad and empty. What will we do now?

We cried a lot, and pushed through the worst period of time we had had since Kelly's departure to Heaven in 2010. (Kelly is our oldest, first born son who was tragically killed in a tractor accident.) So now we had our oldest son in Heaven, and our youngest son in prison. The grief was almost unbearable.

We trusted God every day. We continued to pastor, travel, and be parents and grandparents, and great grandparents. Only through God's strength were we able to persevere.

Cody was incarcerated for 2 and a half years this last time. His testimony is that he needed the extra time in there. This is when God swooped in and saved the day! Cody began to write to us and talk to us about his "calling" and how God was giving him downloads of information and revelation, and he was ready to take off when he was released. He continued to write poems, songs, sermons, and revelations he was receiving. He had opportunity to play instruments a couple times a week. Cody is proficient in guitar and keyboard, and also plays drums with anointing and skill. And he sings.

Cody also met his wife while he was incarcerated in the prison. That is another story!

He is writing his own book, and there is a lot involved with his encounters with the Holy Spirit! I am thankful, and I am proclaiming the faithfulness of God. Our prayer has been that he would follow the call God has had on his life from the womb.

Since Release

Let me begin with this: I now understand that scripture in Ephesians! Verse 20 in Chapter 3 says this: "Now to Him Who, by (in consequence of) the (action of His) power that is at work within us, is able to (carry out His purpose and) do superabundantly far over and above all that we (dare) to ask or think – infinitely beyond our highest prayers, desires, thoughts, hopes or dreams-" (Amplified Bible).

This is our REALITY! I did not even know what that

meant until the Summer of 2018. I thought I did. I have used this scripture over and over for 40 years! NOW I am experiencing the overflowing JOY and the fulfillment of prophetic words spoken so long ago, yet as powerful today as when I heard them for the first time. Our greatest expectation was that Cody would come to church and not do drugs.

We picked Cody up on July 2, 2018. We met friends, Rick and Glenda, for a pizza lunch. Rick and Glenda had invested into his life and had prayed for him consistently. We had a great time of fellowship and prayer. A prophetic word immediately began to unfold.

Friends from Indiana had asked if he could come and testify and share a song he had written at their Celebrate Recovery meeting. We booked him in, and also had plans to do a home bible study and preach in a church in Louisville. Also, a pastor friend from Columbia, Kentucky wanted him to do street meetings with their (recovered from drugs, ex-prisoner – now preacher) son-in-law. So, we had a full schedule planned.

Then the Parole Officer Meeting

Cody is technically "still in prison", and he is serving the rest of his 10-year sentence. He just has the privilege of serving it at home. That is the way it works. He is on Parole. He is not really free, as far as the state is concerned.

His officer met him the next day after release, and told him "absolutely NOT" concerning this ministry trip we had scheduled. He said, maybe in a few months, but not now.

WHAT?????

Time for prayer, time for Father to step in!! I called the PO and spoke with him, and he was explaining all the reasons he could not let Cody leave the state. Mainly, it would be HIS hide (the officer), if something went wrong. He said he had to "get to know" Cody.

I did understand what he was saying. But then I said, "But this is his JOB! We are counting on Cody helping us in this ministry, doing some driving, setting up our tables with products for sale, etc. And, he has appointments to sing and preach."

PO: "Oh, that is different, then, if he will be working and earning money." He asked us to draw up a contract for work, and tell Cody's responsibilities. We drove over to have another meeting and take the paperwork. He gave Cody the travel pass for the whole month of July, because we also had an appointment in Oklahoma.

This was nothing short of miraculous! God was already moving in Cody's life, and ours, and we were bursting with excitement. We had NO IDEA what was about to transpire, or what God had on the agenda!

Preaching, Singing, Beatbox and Miracles

I know I cannot possibly articulate, or even remember all that happened on the trip. It started out anointed, and that spirit continued and multiplied as we went.

On Friday night at the church where the Celebrate Recovery participants were to be, there were also guests and church members, and friends and family who had come to hear Cody. The place was packed! Folks were standing around the walls! I was nervous for him, but he said he was not nervous!

Clifton and I talked to him a little about some do's and don'ts, but basically it was Cody on his own! He dressed up a little, he was so handsome, and he was very confident in what God had given him to talk about. He gave his tremendous testimony, and I was shocked at some things I did not know. (Suicide attempts) He read some word from Romans, and then he sang his song, "Eyes of a Child". He was requested to "beatbox", so he did that, and it was a big hit!

Cody had told us about a word of knowledge (one of the gifts of the Spirit) he had received, and he pushed past his fear of speaking it out. He asked if that fit anyone there? (He was praying "Oh God" ...smile)

Probably twenty hands went up, and 8 of them came to the platform for prayer. The word was about a sleep disorder, although all Cody knew was someone was

12

not sleeping, and he/she would be lying in their bed unable to move, paralyzed with fear. He had never laid hands on and prayed for people before, outside of the jail and prison, and he told them that, but then proceeded to speak deliverance over these people. Many of them have been in touch to say they were completely delivered, and have slept all night ever since that night! He found out this disorder has a name, "Sleep Paralysis". But we found out that the Name of Jesus is above that name!

Home Bible Study
Saturday Night

Clifton and I have had this home bible study for over 30 years back in Indiana. The couple, Kenny and Ellen, have also been married over 50 years, and we have walked through many trials together. Kenny went to India with Clifton in 1989. Ellen gathers the "old group" together when possible. Many have gone on to Heaven.

This meeting was a little different from all our past meetings. The hosts' two adult grandsons were invited so they could hear Cody's testimony and his music. Both of them had similar pasts as Cody, and they both could play music, and they all hit it off in an anointed way. ONLY GOD could have put this together. I am still amazed! We had not seen the boys since they were very young, and I don't think Cody had ever met them before. God had divine appointments for them!

I was able to connect with one of them and he stayed longer just to talk to me and share a dream he had of a scripture. I had a word for him from the Holy Spirit.

This encounter with Cody, and God, and us was answered prayer that these grandparents had gone to God about for years! Let me encourage you that God is on the move in this season of acceleration, and He has given me a word for this season that the believers' adult children are being drawn into His fold, and all our past prayers for them are being answered! GOOD NEWS!

Louisville, KY
The River, and Relatives

Clifton was preaching at The River, Dave Heigl's church. Some of our nieces and nephews live in Louisville, and they have systematically come to visit the church when we are there to hear their uncle preach. There were three of them there the day Cody shared his song, short version of his testimony, and "beatbox".

Cody again shined with the glory of God. His anointing is obvious to anyone who is in tune with the Holy Spirit. It was a glorious day.

It rained out the street meeting in Columbia KY, but we had sweet fellowship with friends, and those who have known Cody since he was a baby. The Relifords have walked through the fire with us when he was in the depths of despair and behaving in a terrible way. We could relate because of the situation with their son-in-law, who also went to prison for drugs, but now is gloriously anointed to sing and preach!

Cody's Ordination was planned at the same time as the 41-year celebration of CCM at the Grace Family Outreach Church, August 2018, whose 12-year anniversary was also being celebrated. We had our most anointed friends and ministers there to speak over Cody and lay hands on him, charging him and setting him apart for the ministry. Clifton then "turned him loose" to preach, sing and beatbox.

After the Ordination we continued to go and preach with Cody and it has been the most glorious time of our ministry! He is also in the new movie coming out hopefully this year!

Cody got married! He met a girl while in prison, a pen pal, and he kept up a phone and letter writing relationship for a whole year before he was released, and then continued after he was released. Cody was offered a great job by a long-time friend, and it worked out perfectly. They have a house and are being responsible adults! They had a simple ceremony in our living room. Welcome ~ Haley ~ to the Coulter family!

We are beyond proud, excited, and looking to the

future for this season of great anointing. Cody has founded and is the leader in a new outreach ministry he holds in the church dining room called "The Love Movement." These young people are recovered, trying, or clean for a while, and some of their parents attend, also. Clifton and I were honored to go and help them celebrate Cody's birthday (he's 31 as of March 17th, St Patrick's Day). It was a surprise party with videos of his people and some minister friends wishing him a happy birthday and giving encouraging words.

As I am doing my final edit in May, 2020, Cody has simply blown us completely away. He is in church every service, on the platform, and not only serves on the worship team, but shares a "nugget" every Sunday before his dad brings the morning message. He preached on LOVE and shared testimony on his Birthday this year which fell on a Sunday!

Cody was injured on his construction job on June 18, 2019. By all physical circumstances, he should have died or been paralyzed. He was under a 1,400-pound wall, setting it with three other men. It shifted and fell on Cody, smashing him, like a flip phone, head between knees, flattened – smushed! (his word) broken back, broken ribs, broken sternum, cartilage ripped from his bones, ankle broken or badly sprained, and inside organs bruised and injured.

As I finish editing this book, I want to say how proud

of Cody we are. He was rushed to ER in an ambulance that day, and the EMT gave him an immediate shot of morphine. He was given a prescription for pain meds and did take that one prescription. He was in excruciating pain after the pills were gone, but Cody refused to get more. He said, "Mom, I don't want what will be waiting down the road if I start this."

Is he still in pain? Yes, he is. BUT... he is also trusting God and moving forward. He will start work in a Recovery Center this month. Perfect Dream Job! He will be doing what he does daily and weekly at the Love Movement for free! He is excited and happy, and so are we!

P.S.
UPDATE! Cody and Haley went to Augusta, Kansas January 2020 to minister, and while praying for people at the end, the Pastor said there was a back being healed. As Cody was driving home (8 hours), he noticed his back was not hurting. He could not drive without pain before! What a mighty God we serve! Cody has remained healed!

I want to encourage you mothers and dads, God has your children! Never give up! Never think your prayers are not working! You, too, will be walking in Ephesians 3:20!

In the beginning of this year, 2020, we saw that Cody's revelation on God's heart exceeded our knowledge and our ability to communicate it. He has been in the pulpit every week, and our church has grown! You need his messages!

CORONAVIRUS UPDATE: We have been coming on Facebook Live with Cody every Sunday morning, and he is doing his Love Movement with the "ZOOM" app online. We have certainly reached a lot of people this way, but of course miss the corporate worship and being together. Our attendance had doubled, and doubled again during the first three months with Cody in the pulpit on Sunday mornings. We are "transitioning" him into taking over the church. We have no plans to retire, but are re-firing for travel and ministry!

Nugget #1
IDENTITY

I was recently invited to teach in two conferences a few months apart on the topic of "Identity". While I have noticed this has been a buzz word in my circles for a few years, I had never zeroed in on the topic individually. This revelation has been something I have weaved into all of my messages.

The "identity" we as Christians, of course, are to identify with is Jesus Christ. I received quite a powerful revelation the morning of my first session on this topic. I had my message, but as I was dressing that morning, putting on my cowgirl boots, the Lord brought to my remembrance a story of a horse Clifton bought a few years ago.

Rain Rot and Hip Bones

Clifton and Kelly (our oldest son who was killed in 2010) had a horse business together, even though Kelly lived in Indiana. Clifton would see a horse at a good price, buy it, and send it to Kelly who fed, broke, trained, showed and sold the horse, and they split the profit.

Clifton went to a local sale barn one Saturday night and came home with the ugliest horse I had ever seen! It was a Palomino mare with rain rot, and so skinny her hip bones stuck out. Hair all matted, mane full of cockle burrs.

I had a fit! "WHY did you spend money on this horse?" Clifton: "I only paid two hundred dollars for her, and you should see her papers!"

Ah, the PAPERS! She was a descendant from a prestigious bloodline! Her DNA screamed talent, power, WINNER! The Lord spoke to me that this is where some of His kids are. We have a negative attitude about ourselves, which causes us to "act" like we are covered with rain rot and cockle burrs. But that is a LIE! Our DNA is extracted from the blood of Jesus! Our bloodline is perfect, victorious, righteous and holy! Our "identity" is parallel with Jesus!

Rain Rot to Trophy!

Let me tell you what happened with the mare. Clifton took her to Kelly, who is my type of God in this story. Kelly took the horse and fed her, doctored her, brushed her, used just the right products on her, and treated her with loving care. When she was "transformed" I did not recognize her. She came to her bloodline's promise. Her DNA rocketed forth. She began to WIN in the show ring. Her identity had been redeemed! Kelly used his great love and talent to train her to bring out the best in her. (Just as God does with us using His Word, and the Word made flesh, JESUS!)

The night before Kelly's tragic, fatal accident, he called me and we had an hour of conversation, covering every base. (It was a gift from God for which I am forever grateful.) During the phone call, he told me about showing the (formerly rain rotted) mare against a $30,000 horse, and our mare WON! The 200-dollar mare won against the 30,000-dollar horse!

YOU HAVE PERFECT DNA

God knew you before you were born. Psalm 139 is a classic declaration of our being known of God before we were even formed in our mother's womb.

Psalm 139:16 (The Passion Translation) *"You saw who you created me to be before I became me."*

This Psalm speaks of God knowing us, having a plan for us, and even writing a book about us! This is our Identity! It is who God has made us!

Romans 8 from TPT is so clear to explain our identity. Look at the second part of verse 3.... *"Yet God sent His Son in human form to **identify** with human weakness."* (Emphasis mine)

I want to try to answer a question that many have at this point. As we *desire* to be like Him and transform into His image, just how do we do that? How do we know when we are "getting there"? I found this in The Passion Translation and was overjoyed! Look!

Romans 8:5
"...*those who live by the **impulses** of the Holy Spirit are motivated to pursue spiritual realities.*"

Then on over in verse 14: "*The mature children of God are those who are moved by the **impulses** of the Holy Spirit.*"

Wow and!!!!!!!

This set me on fire! I immediately thought of the last several times I was MOVED by the impulses of the Holy Spirit! And I remembered the RESULTS of moving in the Holy Spirit!

I was in a place of business recently. The music in there made my spirit grieve, but I was in line to pay so I endured it. When I got to the cash register, I was the only person in the store, and the cashier was the only other person there. His knuckles were bleeding, and as he took my money, I said, "Oh, your hands!" He said, "I know. I burnt them on a heater and they won't heal, because I keep bending them."

He was young, very tattooed, several piercings. A situation I encounter quite often in ministry, and just in everyday life. I am no longer intimidated or fearful of them, because I have learned they are just "people" who need love and encouragement. I said, "May I pray for your hand?"

He stuck it out there and said, "Oh, would you please? My grandmother prays for me."

Let me interject a little nugget teaching here: **Everyone** has a grandmother, an Aunt Esther, a cousin, an uncle, *someone* they know who prays! The enemy of our souls wants us to think these people who look different from us are hard and will spit on us or something...cuss us out...whatever. But NO! This will not happen! They are glad you are going to pray for them!

So, I was able to lay hands on his hand and pray. Then I found out he knows Cody, and I invited him to the Love Movement, and he had already heard of it, and was glad to know I was Cody's mother. He apologized for the music that was on. It was a radio station the boss wants left on, he said.

Another example I have recently encountered is a gas station attendant who was also tattooed, ring piercings everywhere...tongue, eye, lip. I was led to say, "Has anyone told you today that Jesus loves you?"

He looked at me, shocked, and said, "No! I'm not a Christian." I said, 'Oh. Well God loves you anyway. I pray that you see His favor in your life today." He was a very handsome young man, and I perceived that God was after his heart.

The next time I went in, I said, "Oh, you're the one who Jesus loves." He looked at me and said, "I want to tell you how much I appreciated what you said to me. I have never had anyone say that to me."

It is simple. He does not know his identity. I will never stop saying these things to people. He will eventually come to Jesus, I know it! I have planted, I have watered, maybe I will harvest, or maybe someone else will, but all glory goes to God the Father, no matter what!

We Are Beloved of God!

Now back to the teaching from Romans. What is a "mature" Christian? It is someone who knows who we are and what we have.

In Ephesians – the first chapter alone – we are tagged as being just absolutely awesome! We are beloved! We are blessed, have obtained an inheritance, we are unblameable, have been made holy, we are chosen, ordained, we have redemption, and have received every spiritual blessing in heavenly places! We have been given *"super abundant grace"* (TPT), we have wisdom, understanding, and revelation. And we have been *"stamped with the seal of His Holy Spirit of promise*!" This first chapter also declares that Paul is praying we "continually experience the immeasurable greatness of God's power made available to you through faith".

When we "know" God is this way, we are confident that He will always back us up.

I personally got to "know" God through adversity. I had already been in ministry with my husband for 7 years when we encountered horrendous opposition. The enemy of our souls came to kill, steal, and destroy us and our ministry. I had to find out who I was, and who God was. I had no one to help me. I had the Holy Ghost showing up every day, then every hour, then it seemed every single minute of the day to help me. I got to know HIM! It was hell on earth to walk through such devastation, but I would not trade the relationship I developed with the Spirit of God for anything.

There's Power in the Word!

For people to learn "who they are", their "identity", we must go to the Word of God.

Romans 12:2 (KJV), "*And be not conformed to this world, but be ye transformed by the renewing of your mind, that ye may prove what is that good, and acceptable, and perfect will of God.*"

Our minds must be renewed on the word of God if we are going to be transformed. I heard someone preach that Jesus did not die on the cross so we could "go to Heaven," but rather so that we would be transformed into His image. No other way can we be transformed into His image, but by renewing our minds on His word.

There is power in the word of God. In John 1:1 we read, "*In the beginning was the Word, and the Word was with God and the Word was God.*" In verse 14 it says, "*And the Word was made flesh and dwelt among us, (and we beheld His glory, the glory as of the only begotten of the Father,) full of grace and truth.*"

Jesus said of His words, "*they are Spirit and they are life.*" (see John 6:63)

There is so much power in the word of God. I want to tell you something that is happening as I am editing and finishing this book here in early 2019. A few months ago, I was cut out of someone's life – a dearly beloved family member. It is actually someone I love passionately, and have helped his whole life. He is in a serious situation, and I was trying to counsel him. He finally told me he did not want to hear from any of us. The whole family was cut off.

As heartbreaking as this was, I knew he really did not mean it. I left it alone for a while, but after our family pictures were taken, I decided to try again to reach out by sending family pictures, a letter, a Christmas card, and of course money. While I did receive a generic response, it was cold and uncaring. I felt a sense from the Holy Spirt, "Send him My Word." And I felt a strong leading to certain scriptures. I wrote them out and sent them. I continued every day to send the Word of God, the specific ones He was leading me to send. My loved one responded with amazing words! He told me the scriptures I sent were exactly what he needed, and that it sounded just like what he felt in his heart. (It was the Psalmist David crying out from the cave, and other times of deep despair.) But then you know how David always pulls himself up by his bootstraps and ends up in a Praise mode. My loved one told me he went to the chapel. He said he was the only one in there and he went to the front of the church and talked to God!

This was ONLY BECAUSE OF GOD'S WORD!!! (And me being brave due to God's own power and strength.)

Hebrews 4:12 (KJV) *"For the word of God is quick, powerful, and sharper than any two-edged sword, piercing even to the dividing asunder of soul and spirit, and of the joints and marrow, and is a discerner of the thoughts and intents of the heart."*

The life is in the blood. The blood is in the marrow. The joints, the bone, is covering the marrow. The Word of God can divide that so sharply that the blood can flow. Our bone here represents the soul. Just as the scripture said, the WORD of God is so sharp that it divides that bone from marrow. The life – spirit – longs to flow from the inside out to the outside. The soul realm is our will, our emotions, our fears, our seat of personality and our minds. The soul is like a bone, hardness, not willing that the life blood should flow. BUT THE WORD of God can cut right through there and cause the life blood to flow to people who need it. As we recognize our "Identity" as a son or daughter of God, we will use the word of God to rightly divide the bone from the marrow, the thoughts and intents of the heart will flow.

I see this so clearly, but can only hope I get the revelation across! Never forget how quick (alive) and powerful the word of God is.

Be Renewed in Your Attitude

The other scripture I use in most of my messages is the one in Ephesians 4. Verse 23 says, *"And be renewed in the spirit of your mind."* The verses surrounding this verse are saying to put off the old man and put on the new man. When we are "renewed" in our minds, we are renewed in our attitude! Being renewed in our attitude is vital to life. Most of what you are living is due to your attitude about it. Are you broke? What is your attitude? "Oh, I'm broke, I don't have any money, how am I going to pay my bills? How am I going to live?"

Renewing your mind to the Word of God will cause you to switch to, "Well, Lord, I know I am slim on finances right now, but Your word says you supply all my needs, and I have plenty, that Your paths drip with abundance, and I am on Your path, Lord, so I am expecting my finances to increase and I expect You to fill the empty places and cause me to prosper."

Are you sick? What are you saying? Your identity is that you are the healed of the Lord. See the healing chapter in this book. Speak the Truth that the Word of God teaches.

Learning our identity in Jesus releases us from fear and dread and self-destruction.

Understanding our place in God's kingdom, His divine Plan for us, discovering His love for us releases the insecurity and jealousy we may be harboring.

There is never a valid reason to be insecure or jealous of anything anyone has, because God has the perfect plan for you, individually! Seek His face today and ask Him about your identity! He will assure you, by the power of His spirit, that you are His beloved. Ask Him to reveal Himself to you, and He will!

Nugget #2
MARRIAGE

God's plan for marriage is for us to have a "Heaven on Earth" relationship. God was so happy and excited when He made man and woman and put them together to enjoy life with each other and with Him. God thought what He had made was "*very good.*" (Genesis 1:31)

Some of you are wondering, "Really? What happened?" And rightfully so. Many reading this are either "existing" – riding it out because you have been married for so long – or some are thinking, "Why not just keep this one, it is too hard to go into the dating scene again." Many married people are not happy today, yet God desires for us to be full of joy! Are you taking your marriage for granted? The husband and the wife are to be "cherished" by each other. God has promised His children a "*land like the days of heaven on earth.*" (Deuteronomy 11:21) My own marriage was healed, put back better than before, and God will do it for anybody who is willing to listen to Him and make the changes He leads you to make. (And turn from selfishness.)

As a disclaimer – I want to, from the start, let everyone know that there is no condemnation here. If you are divorced, you can't get "un-divorced." We have to start where we are, and go from here. Divorce happens every day, even to Christians. It is not God's best, (most of the time) but it is not the unpardonable sin. Divorce is forgivable, just as is every other sin except unbelief. We must start on a level field. You are forgiven, blessed, highly favored, and a child of the Most High!

I was taught marriage, God's way, by the Lord Himself. The principles I learned and applied healed my marriage many years ago. No matter where you are in your marriage relationship, even if it is a great marriage, there will be some "nugget" in this chapter you can apply that will make your relationship better. In the days I was fighting for my marriage, I had heard no teaching on marriage, and neither did I have any books or tapes on the subject. One day a set of tapes fell into my hands, and helped me tremendously. I began to teach the truths God showed me, and the principles I learned, and have seen many marriages healed. Clifton and I traveled across the United States and around the world doing couples conferences and seeing miracles. The greatest miracle on earth is the turning around of a heart. We have witnessed couples literally on the verge of divorce come back to a happy, healthy marriage. One couple came – over 40 years ago – to a conference we were doing in Kansas City. The husband was leaving – on his way out of town – when he turned around and came back for the "Marriage Encounter" we were conducting in the church. They are celebrating over 40 years of marriage now. Happy, blessed, compatible, and at peace. That's what God can and will do if He has some cooperation!

New Beginnings

Many of us today need a "new beginning" in our marriages. New beginnings are available every single day, and God has one for you. Even if your marriage is wonderful, these nuggets will open some new revelation.

God gave us all a new beginning when He sent Jesus to the earth. It was a new beginning for all mankind. This "good news" is preached today, and it gives every man, woman, and child a chance for a brand-new life. I needed a new beginning when I got saved. And since that time, I have needed, and have received new beginning after new beginning. Every day we have the first brand new day of the rest of our lives. Only through the Spirit of the living God can this happen! If you have not heard this before, call on His name, and you will be saved! (see Romans 10:13) Pray: "Jesus, I believe, I'm sorry for my sin, and I want You in my life, come into my heart". Now just thank Him for your new life. My first new beginning happened when I was born again.

The new beginning that God has made available to us through the birth, life, death, and resurrection of Jesus changes our lives forever. Our only requirement is to receive it. Once we receive what God has offered as a free gift, it causes us to walk through a door where nothing is impossible to us, and since He gave Jesus, the Bible says *"will He not freely give us all things?"* (Romans 8:32) The answer is YES, He will, and has already given us all things. The first decision that needs to be made in pursuing a good marriage is, PUT JESUS FIRST. Anything less will not produce a good marriage. Clifton and I, after years of counseling couples for hours at a time, cut it down to this: "Where is Jesus in your life?" And if they cannot tell us that God is first place, that is what we work on first. They would have to come to church for at least 6 weeks in a row if we were going to sit with them and work through their issues. Sitting under the anointing of the Spirit of God will change anything needing to be changed if we will open up and receive.

When I was fighting for my marriage, God supernaturally placed teachings into my hands, and led me to specific scriptures, and He sovereignly walked me through the hardest season of my life up until that time. I never said a word to anybody about what was happening. This journey was a walk into the unknown, and it was only the two of us, just me and God. Me and the Holy Ghost. That period of time was when I got to know God for who He is, and saw what He would do. I thought I was a faith woman, but it was not until I saw my husband transform before my eyes that I understood faith. And I understood many concepts of marriage, and the covenant involved with two becoming one. These principles work for both the man and the woman. Husband and wife. They are Kingdom Principles. Unconditional Love works!

I Will Restore

After my husband actually told me he did not love me, was leaving and getting a divorce, I had to face the sobering truth that I worshiped my husband, and had put him first in my life. I thought I had placed God on the throne of my heart, but when my husband said these things to me, I felt lost, alone, and totally by myself. I realized that I needed to find the will of God for myself. I became intimate with the Lord through this valley. "Intimacy" became my foundation for Christian life and ministry. Intimacy with the heart of God.

One of the first scriptures He led me to read and meditate upon was Joel 2:25-26.

"I will restore to you the years that the locust has eaten... and you shall eat in plenty, and be satisfied, and praise the name of the Lord your God, that has dealt wondrously with you: and my people shall never be ashamed."

I grabbed that verse and hung on for dear life! It was supernaturally illuminated to me. It was a "rhema" word, a word that I knew was from God to me, personally.

Notice He said He would restore years. I needed years restored, and many reading this chapter need years restored. God showed me that restoration – God's way – meant "bigger, better, and more than what was lost, stolen, or taken away." I read this somewhere, and it stuck.

Look at what this says: "*God has dealt wondrously with **YOU**.*" (emphasis mine) I wanted God to deal wondrously with my husband! It was then that I got down on my knees and I earnestly prayed, "Lord, if there is anything I need to change, please show me." We all have a tendency to want God to change the other person. "God, change my employer, God, change my kids, God, change my friend." He wants to change **us**. We can never change anyone but ourselves. God does not want you to change for HIM, but it is for your good that He wants you to change to be more conformed to His image.

The God Kind of Wife

That prayer took me on a journey I was not expecting! God began to gently show me my shortcomings as far as being a wife and help meet. It was not a pretty sight! I was crushed, but I knew it was the truth. I opened up to the Holy Spirit and I let him do surgery on me.

This passage also says that "*my people shall never be ashamed.*" I felt I was about to be ashamed any minute, but if the word of God said His people would not be ashamed, then I claimed that for myself. Now, remember, I was a Pastor's wife! Every Sunday after Clifton preached, I thought, "Wow, he is going to go home and love me now." He preached good! But when we got home, it was just like before.

The Lord began to teach me how to be a wife. I started sharing these truths on my daily radio broadcast. My series was entitled, "The God Kind of Wife."

Let's look at Paul's letter to the Ephesians, Chapter 5. This book is filled with powerful words, and especially about marriage. The Apostle Paul begins this chapter with instruction about walking in love. He is speaking to the church here. We are to be "followers of God, as dear children." Verse 2 says, "*And walk in love, as Christ also has loved us, and has given Himself for us an offering and a sacrifice to God for a sweet-smelling savor.*" If we renew our minds and actions to the things Paul taught the church, the body of Christ, this will heal any marriage.

Walking in love is the key to success in life. Not that we walk in our own love, but knowing that God truly loves us with an everlasting, never ending love causes us to be able to love others. And it is the key to success in marriage. As God opened my eyes to the fact that I needed to change, it was most difficult. No one wants to change. I knew, however, that if God and I were going to save this marriage, I had to allow Him to make this worm (me) a butterfly!

Submission? Oh No!

When I got to verse 22 on *"Wives, submit yourselves to your own husbands, as unto the Lord"*, I thought I was submissive, so I almost skipped on by that one. The Lord stopped me cold and showed me the truth. (Remember I had ASKED Him to show me where I needed to change.) I did not know at that time in the early 1980's what this scripture really meant. I was a student of searching out things, but had not yet done research on this scripture. I took it at face value, and did not know what was ahead for me. God revealed to me that I was only submissive when I wanted to be. ("Really God?!") This covered all areas of our lives, even small things like popcorn. If Clifton would ask me to pop popcorn, I only did it when I wanted popcorn. If I did not want popcorn, nobody got popcorn! And there were no microwaves. Popping corn required standing at the stove. If I was too tired, no, I just did not do it. This is an example, but it spanned across every area of our lives. I was shown by my loving Father that I needed to be more attentive to my husband, and less attentive to my girlfriends and church related activities. "Ouch!"

In the verse before verse 22, we see verse 21 which is the key to good relationships. *"Submitting yourselves one to another in the fear of God."* The word fear here is "reverence." It does not hurt us to defer to other people's wishes when there is an opportunity to have a difference of opinion. Paul said to "pursue peace."

This is the one verse we eventually focused on to heal our marriage, but first I had to take some drastic measures if I wanted to keep my marriage. And I did.

From verses 23 to 33 we read about the husband and the wife. These are anointed scriptures, filled with life and power. The Apostle Paul is relating the way Jesus is with us, the church, and he even makes it plainer when he said, in verse 32, *"This is a great mystery: but I speak concerning Christ and the church."* This reflection of Jesus and the CHURCH, as compared to the husband and wife is more than we can comprehend as human beings. It takes the Spirit to unveil the depth and width of this revelation. Pray to go deeper with this relevant truth. Then in verse 33 he closes this portion with, *"Nevertheless, let every one of you in particular so love his wife even as himself; and the wife see that she reverences her husband."* I learned that the wife needs love and the husband needs respect. And he does not say, "if they deserve it."

The Amplified Bible says:

"However let each man of you (without exception) love his wife as [being in a sense] his very own self; and let the wife see that she respects and reverences her husband – that she notices him, regards him, honors him, prefers him, venerates and esteems him; and that she defers to him, praises him, and loves and admires him exceedingly."

What a dynamite verse! I worked on this for months. I did these things. I took the word of God seriously. I began to praise my husband in the midst of a static, troubled relationship. I heard a lot of whining when I would present this verse to women. It is not easy or fun in the beginning. However! As we become a "doer of the Word", God moves in power to change the mind and heart of a husband.

Some women told me there was "nothing" to praise the husband for. I counseled ladies to take a sheet of blank paper and draw a line down through the middle, and write on one side her husband's weaknesses, and on the other side his strengths. Sometimes we had to start on the strengths side with: "He works a job." So, she had this to praise him for. "Honey, I am so happy that you work every day, and that you provide for this family. Thank you so much for that. We appreciate your diligence in caring for us." As this practice is followed, a change begins.

I received testimonials, and I can testify myself, that this works. Love changes people. It changed my husband, and it will change yours!

People say, "It takes two." I was the only one desiring to fix the marriage. My husband was "done", and threatening to go to the lawyer to file for divorce. I had no one to talk to, no help, nothing but the Bible and the Holy Ghost! Eventually it does take both husband and wife in agreement to have a great marriage, but it can start with just one human and one Holy Spirit!

I heard someone say one time to say "Praise the Lord" every time you pick up your husband's dirty socks or underwear. Reason number one, that you have a good, strong back to pick them up, secondly that you have a husband, because there is someone who would like to have your husband. You may say, "Not MY husband!" YES, your husband! Because of this fact, there is another tip I will give now: Ladies, don't be running around the house in you robe he saw you in when he left for work! There are plenty of females at his work place who dress up like they are going to a fashion show. Not necessarily office girls, but also in factories, or anywhere! They wear make-up, fix their hair, and look beautiful. Then your husband comes home and you are looking like the last rose of summer in your house shoes and uncombed hair. It makes a difference. Your husband wants you to look nice. He wants to be appreciated; he wants respect. These are simple "doable" little things that make a BIG difference.

Don't Argue

As I praised my husband when he was trying to do everything, he could to make me hate him, (he admitted he was doing this) I began to see a change. I started putting him first in relationships. I already know all the arguments that you would try to tell me in regards to why you can't do this. "I can't honor him. He is non-honorable!" Or from a man's standpoint, "You don't understand how she treats me." That's when we turn to God and ask Him for help. He would never have had the Apostle Paul write such outrageous instructions if we were unable to carry them out. YES, it hurts! YES, you want to scream! The question is, "Do you want to save your marriage?"

God's word is the only power in the universe that can bring something dead back to life. Following the plan of God will yield results quickly in some areas, and maybe not so fast in others, but hope will spring up when even one glimpse of change appears. I walked this out without seeing any change for a long time. I cooked his favorite food, I kept his clothes ready at all times, and I DID NOT ARGUE. I spoke positive statements always. I told him I loved him, knowing I was not going to hear it back.

His testimony is that one day God spoke to him to tell

me he loved me. Even though he did not "feel" it, he did it. This was a start for him, and in the end, he FELT more love for me than he ever had before. This has lasted now for over 35 years! We had been married about 17 years at the time.

"Shut Up"

The Spirit of the Lord spoke to me one day, and I heard as clear as a bell, "Shut up. Stop arguing with your husband. Let him rant and rave, or say whatever he wants to say. Your response is to be silent, or when appropriate, I will tell you what to say."

Life changer! "*Where there is no wood the fire goes out.*" (Proverbs 26:20) So, that was the end of the arguments. Major power tool. One person cannot argue with himself. I would go into the bathroom and pray in tongues. Sometimes I was not praying, I was letting off steam! Did you know you can let off steam in tongues? Yes!

During this time period we were on our way to a revival where my husband was preaching. He was trying to argue before we got there. He was mad at me. I don't remember why, but it seemed he was always mad at me. He found something wrong with me every day. Clifton stopped the car and told me to get out. I got out and started walking down the highway. In those days church women wore panty hose, high heels, and most definitely a dress. He drove beside me, begging me to get back in the car, then turned around and came back, and kept trying to get me to get in. There was NO WAY I was getting back in that car! He drove on. Finally, the people on their way to the revival were passing me, and someone recognized me, and came back and asked me if I needed a ride. Yes, I did. I am sure that little incident was just what Clifton needed to feel the anointing at the meeting. I throw this in to let you know that this was no cake walk! We both made mistakes. We were both passionate, strong, and believed we were right!

Back to "Submission."

In I Peter 3 (KJV) again we read that the wife is to submit to her husband. Listen to how interesting this is, "*Likewise ye wives, be in subjection to your own husbands; that if any obey not the word, they may also without the word be won by the conversation of the wives*."

During this period of being young in the word, I did not know that in this scripture the word "conversation" meant "way of life". All I had was the King James version of the Bible. I thought if I was talking on the phone, I should say things that I could not say to the husband, but if he overheard, he would be won over! (I know that sounds crazy!)

But, alas, I got the meaning, and taught this to others

as I was practicing what I was learning. Peter goes on to say, (KJV) *"While they behold your chaste conversation, coupled with fear."* He was saying that as the husband watches his wife's pure way of life, he will have a reverence for her and for God. This 3rd chapter is another powerful set of words, anointed of the Holy Ghost to bring change.

Verse 4, *"But let it be the hidden man of the heart, in that which is not corruptible, even the ornament of a meek and quiet spirit, which is in the sight of God of great price."*

I was taken aback when I read that part about a "meek and quiet spirit", because I was not meek or quiet, as I saw meek and quiet. In reality, meek is "teachable" and the quiet spirit I did have, even though I questioned that one. I was quiet in my spirit when I was listening to my Father. That is what He showed me.

There are 6 verses (1-6) to the wives in 1 Peter 3. One verse to the husbands, (verse 7) to "honor" her. Peter says that the husband's prayers are hindered if he does not get along with his wife. Heavy duty.

God Will Meet You

I have said before in testimony that I was "mincemeat" when the Lord was finished with me, after I had prayed the prayer for Him to show me my shortcomings. I honestly thought He would say, "Geri, you are doing everything right, it is Clifton who needs to change." God lovingly took me by the hand, and not only showed me where I needed to change some behaviors to please my husband, but He led me to a place of peace and confidence that if I would listen to Him, He would do the rest. And He did. God will meet you and lead you.

Let's talk about "submission". It became a dirty word in the 1980's because some teachers and preachers took it to the extreme, and I know some horror stories of this biblical application where it was pathetically perverted.

My husband is a good man, and was a good man then, and being "submissive" towards him, as I believed I was supposed to be at that time, was not grievous for me. However, as I taught this principle, women were coming to my office with stories that were neither godly nor scriptural. I had to dig into the teaching, dig into the scriptures! God would never have His daughters mistreated, just like we as parents would not allow our own children to be abused or molested. Some of the "submission" error was taught like this: "You as a wife obey your husband no matter what, and he will stand before God for the wrongdoing, not you." NOT RIGHT! There was great damage done to women during that time period. I was saddened by it then, and I still am to this day.

For one thing, don't forget verse 21, directly above the one on wives submitting. "*Submitting yourselves one to another, in the fear of God.*" The pearl of great price here is "love". Deferring in love is a godly attribute.

When the husband loves his wife like Christ loved the church and gave Himself for it, there is never a conflict! Clifton would say "submit!" I would say, "Love me like Christ loved the church." He said, "I do, the denominational church". Which at that time we knew only as a cold, dead institution. He was kidding. We have always laughed at ourselves, and he has a sense of humor in the midst of conflict. Laughter is good. Clifton always keeps me laughing. Laughing at ourselves is vital for our emotional and physical health.

Love Came to Live in Us

When love came to live in us, we began to love each other like the Lord had in mind. Always preferring the other, esteeming the other. When we read the New Testament, and see how Paul taught the church to relate to each other, it is just simple Christianity, and the way a husband and wife should relate to one another. Our homes should operate as Paul gave instruction for the church to function. Selfishness has to go by the wayside as we prefer the other. We can trace almost any problem in marriage to "selfishness." Pride. God calls for "Self-LESS-ness." Yes, it hurts the ole pride and it hurts to not get your way. But we all have to make a decision about what we want – our own way, or a godly marriage?

I also studied in depth the Virtuous Woman from Proverbs 31:10-31, and tried to be her. She is Super Woman, but a goal to reach for. Later in life, I realized that SHE is the CHURCH. I have a nugget on that!

After I had done these things I have mentioned, and sought the Lord with all my heart, Andrew Wommack came to our church to minister in a big tent meeting. Clifton had told our right-hand man that after Andrew left, he was leaving, and to destroy all his tapes from the previous years of ministry.

We had told Andrew nothing about our marriage. We had only just met him. One day at lunch he looked across the table at Clifton, and he said, "You are about to make the biggest mistake of your life." Then he proceeded to tell us about a "Minister's Marriage Conference" he was having the next month, and invited us as his guests. That is a long story, but the short version is, we did go, and our marriage was turned around. All the seed I had planted was harvested at that set of meetings. We still had some rough roads after we got home, but in the end, we fell in love more than ever, and God gave us a "consolation prize" (Clifton's words) – a new baby! Now, over 30 years later we are the loves of each other's lives.

Forgiveness

Something important is to always forgive. Forgiveness is a must for a good marriage, or any human relationship. If a deep wound has been caused, sometimes the pain is overwhelming, and causes our breath to be sucked out of us. But worse is unforgiveness. Unforgiveness paralyzes us. To "feel" the forgiveness may take time, but we plant it as a seed as we read about in Luke 17. Jesus was teaching His disciples about forgiveness in the first four verses, then they said to Jesus, "Increase our faith." He said:

"If you have faith as a mustard seed, you can say to this mulberry tree, 'Be pulled up by the roots and be planted in the sea' and it would obey you."

I learned this, and it has helped me. When we forgive, we want to feel it immediately. Sometimes the transgression against us is great. We have pain we can't control. We don't "feel" as if we have forgiven, because we still have a broken heart. Then we find ourselves under condemnation. No, just go to your Father and say to Him that you forgive. Sow a seed. HIS power will kick in and before you know it, you can actually feel the love and forgiveness for your spouse. Tell him/her you forgive. This is not based at all on feelings, but on faith in God's word. This works outside of marriage also, in any human relationship.

Concerning those other than your spouse, you will be

able hear that person's name without feeling nauseated. God will also protect you from seeing the person or persons who hurt you so deeply until you are ready to face them. He is so good to us! He loves the person who hurt you, too.

To Wives: What if There is Another Woman? Husbands: What can I do?

I heard CM Ward talking about this on TBN decades ago, and he said some wives go to bed in curlers, a nightgown from their necks to the floor, and reading the Pentecostal Evangel! (This was a magazine in the 70's that spoke of the happenings in the world of Pentecost. Smile.) He was making the point that these overly "religious" women wondered why their husbands strayed. He said to the wives: "Find out what he is attracted to in the other woman and be her!"

I can tell you that a husband wants to be the hero. He wants to be the one his wife looks to, depends on, and pays attention to. As busy wives, young mothers and business or working women, it is a difficult task to spin all the plates. However, a valuable tip is to *make time* for your husband. Praise him, set aside time for him, go with him when he asks you to, whether it is to fish (you hate fishing), or even hunt, or just go to Bass Pro Shop to look around. A little thing like that can make a huge difference in your relationship.

The Adulteress

There is a woman out there who would love to have your husband. The adulteress woman gets her ducks in a row and sets her trap. Solomon taught us about her in the Proverbs. Chapter 5 says that her lips drip honey, and her mouth is smoother than oil, but in the end, she is bitter as wormwood. Wormwood was a drug in ancient times that when chewed caused insanity. Solomon said her feet go down to death; her steps lay hold of hell. Her ways are unstable.

The wisest man who ever lived says to stay away from her! Don't go near her! He who does, will be mourning in the end. This whole Chapter 5 is dealing with this subject. He continues:

"Drink waters from your own cistern, And running water from your own well. Should your fountains be dispersed abroad, Streams of water in the streets? Let them be only your own, And not for strangers with you. Let your fountain be blessed, And rejoice with the wife of your youth."

Clearly, he is speaking of the husband sticking with his wife! He goes on to say..."*Always be enraptured with her love.*"

When Clifton said he did not love me, I said, "Oh, yes, you are enraptured with me!" (One translation says "ravished". I used that word, "You are ravished with my love!")

In Chapter 7 Solomon tells the story of the adulteress woman who says – verse 14 – "*I have peace offerings with me, I have paid my vows.*" This woman is not the woman at the bars or the casino. No, she is your everyday sister in the local congregation. She is your friend. She is the secretary, she is the Sunday School teacher, the piano player. The rest of the chapter expounds on her ways and her thought processes to lure and to entice.

"*I have spread my bed with tapestry, Colored coverings of Egyptian linen. I have perfumed my bed With myrrh, aloes, and cinnamon. Come, let us take our fill of love until morning; Let us delight ourselves with love. For my husband is not at home; He has gone on a long journey.*"

One thing to notice here, the adulteress (married woman) is not doing this for money, like the harlot. She is bored. She decides to have some excitement in her life, since her boring husband is away making a living for his family. She pays no attention to whether her prey has a wife, children, or a home.

This chapter goes ahead to say that she seduces him with her flattery until finally a dart strikes him in his liver. "He did not know it would cost him his life."

If the wife discovers her husband is having an affair,

she has to get in the Spirit and fight this with the power of God. Most couples just throw in the towel when there is unfaithfulness, but God can bring the dead to life! God can cause dead love to be resurrected. I try to get couples to see the value of the time they have invested, and the history, and the potential future of their marriage! Things must be done God's way for them to work. He has made it that way, HIS WORD is Spirit and Life!

Wives who find other men to spend time with are also deceived and led astray by lust. Sometimes, though, they are just wanting someone to pay attention to them. They want to be told they are loved. One man actually said, "I told her that when we got married." We told him he needed to say it again!

Husbands need to apply the word of God. We have witnessed many impossible marriages receive total healing. Often times a counselling session and sitting under the anointed word of God for a season is a healing balm.

Never Say Divorce

Don't give the enemy any fuel for his fire. One thing I learned from a veteran of the faith is to "never say divorce." When my husband said "divorce", I ignored it, and when he said he did not love me I said, "Yes, you do, you are just deceived. You are ravished with my love." He looked at me like I was crazy, but that is what I always said. Words are powerful, and I was led by the Spirit to speak only positive, spirit-filled words.

After a while, (a long while), our marriage was made bigger, better, more of what we had lost. God did it. But we had to cooperate with Him and follow His instruction. New beginnings are available to us every day. His mercies are new every morning! I pray you have seen something valuable to apply to your home and family.

Remember, marriage is to be a picture of "heaven on earth".

And a P.S. ~ If we as believers strive to follow the word of God put forth by the Apostle Paul concerning the way we are to treat each other as members of the church, we will get along fine in our homes!

Nugget #3

BOOK OF RUTH

Rise Up!
Chapter 1

The book of Ruth is the eighth book of the bible. The number 8 is God's number for "new beginnings." The seventh book is Judges. Seven is God's number for completion. God made the earth in 6 days. The 7th day was a day of rest. The work was done. Day number 8 was a new beginning.

At the end of the book of Judges the last verse states, "In those days there was no king in Israel; everyone did what was right in his own sight." The very next verse, which is the first verse of the book of Ruth says this: "Now, it came to pass in the days when the judges ruled, that there was a famine in the land." So, this makes me think when men are doing what is right in their own sight, there will be a famine. (Are you experiencing a famine, or lack in any area of your life today? Are you doing what is right in our own eyes, or are you seeking God's will for your life? I had to think about this. I teach it all around the world.)

A man named Elimelech (Name means "My God is King") took his wife, Naomi, (Pleasant, Delightful, Lovely) and sons, Mahlon (Weak, Sickly), Chilion (Failing and Pining) to Moab.   The word here is "sojourn" (KJV), he took them to sojourn. This word denotes that he was taking them to "temporarily dwell" because of the famine. In the end he stayed. The bible says he "continued" there, and his sons grew up and married Moabite women. The Moabites, though they married Jewish men, were not allowed into the congregation of Israel until the 10th generation.   The wives' names were Orpha and Ruth.   Orpah means "Fawn" and Ruth is "Friend".

After Naomi's husband and sons died, she was left with her two daughters-in-law in the land of Moab, a land of strange gods and idols. Moab means "covetousness, greed, and idolatry." In verse 6 of Chapter 1 we read, speaking of Naomi, "Then she arose" ... verse 7, "...she went out from the place where she was....". I will make a point here that if we are going to have a new beginning, we must arise. We must go forth from the place where we are presently. The four lepers in II Kings 7:3 (KJV) asked a profound question, "Why sit we here till we die?" That's what I thought one day, and I got up and went from the place where I was. I stopped sitting where I was, and hence received a new beginning!   To receive a new beginning, you must be really fed up to the top with your situation and circumstances.   It takes courage and it takes faith to change. God will be a tremendous help, though, don't underestimate Him in your move. To be more exact, He will do it all, with a little cooperation from you. It only takes a "little faith", mustard seed size, not a lot of faith.

Naomi "heard", the bible says, that there was bread again in her homeland. Your relatives, your family will always "hear" about good news. They will know when you are doing well, even when they have chosen to go to a place of wilderness. This will give them a hope and a sense that something good can happen to them.

Naomi decided to "arise", or RISE UP. Ruth went with her mother-in-law back to Bethlehem – Judah, "House of Bread", and "House of Praise". Ruth did not know what she was getting into. She only knew she wanted Naomi's people to be her people, and Naomi's God to be her God. Naomi was a type of God to Ruth. Even though Naomi had some "negative confessions" upon her return to her city, Ruth had evidently seen a strong faith and a deep commitment from Naomi concerning this God she served. When she got to Bethlehem, the whole town said, "Is this Naomi?" Ruth 1:20-21: "And she said to them, 'Call me not Naomi (pleasant), call me Mara (bitter); for the Almighty has dealt very bitterly with me. I went out full, and the Lord has brought me home again empty.'..." I have wondered about this scripture, and thought, "Why would Ruth follow a bitter woman"? Then as I meditated, and saw what kind of woman Naomi was, I saw that she might have had thoughts of "affliction", because she did go on to say that the Lord had afflicted her in that verse. However, her character was one of utmost integrity, and she had Ruth's best interest in her heart. She loved Ruth, and had to have been the best mother-in-law ever, to have had this kind of loyalty shown to her. Just because we read something in the Bible, does not mean that is the way it is. I mean by that, Naomi said the Lord had afflicted her, but she was mistaken. God is never mistaken, but our perception of Him is often mistaken. It is not God who afflicts us, ever. It is God who has given us all things, and has blessed us with favor and love.

Faith and Favor
Chapter 2

They arrived back in Bethlehem at the beginning of barley harvest. "Timing" is everything in the plan of God. "My times are in His hands," says the Psalmist David. (Psalm 31:15) We get out of timing and mess things up. When the timing chain goes bad in your vehicle, you aren't going anywhere. Spin, spin, spin. How many of us have been sitting spinning because we got out of the plan of God's timing? I can be a witness to it, sadly. Don't count God out though, He is ever faithful to fix it for you, and give you a new beginning! For Ruth and Naomi to arrive in town just in time for the barley harvest is significant in the history of the world. Naomi sent Ruth out to "glean" and the bible says that Ruth "happened to light" on a field belonging to Boaz. And it's off to the races!! We know that she landed on the field of Boaz by Divine guidance.

"Gleaning" was a practice in that day intended for the purpose of sustaining the poor. The landowners would instruct their reapers to leave the corners of the rectangular fields for the gleaners to harvest the grain for their day's food and living.

When Boaz saw Ruth there, he asked his servant, who was in charge of the reapers, "**Who** is this woman?" (Emphasis mine) The reaper explained that this was the Moabite who came back from Moab with Naomi. He said Moab twice to make sure Boaz knew the woman was not of their people. There was prejudice in that day, just as there is today.

Boaz knew immediately that he was a "KINSMAN REDEEMER." This woman, Ruth, had been married to his relative, and the custom was that he would marry her, and raise up a son to carry on the name of the family, if he was the closest relative.

The servant told Boaz that she had come and asked if she could glean, and that she had been there from morning till now. She had "continued", the bible says. This shows diligence on Ruth's part. She came to a strange place, with strange people, but was determined to work to take care of her mother-in-law. Boaz liked this about her, and even said he had heard she was being good to Naomi. (Let me tell you, others will "hear" that you are preaching the gospel of truth. They will hear that you are a person of love and remember when they need help.)

At that time, he asked Ruth to listen to him, and not go to glean in any other field. He told her to stay close to his young women. I believe we are to stick with Jesus, and not try to glean from any other field, but make Him our One and Only. "Let your eyes be on the field....", He said.   We are to keep our eyes on the field of people's hearts and on the field of the heart of our Lord.

Ruth was so grateful that she fell on her face and bowed to the ground thanking him and wondering out loud "Why have I found favor in your eyes...?" He then mentioned her good works towards Naomi and that she had left all she knew to be there. May I say here that as a type of Jesus, we can see His love and heart towards those who are caring about others, especially family. Another thing I noticed here is that Ruth is so like we are today. In verse 2 she said to Naomi that she wanted to "find favor" in whose sight she would glean. Then when she did find that favor she asked for, she was amazed, and couldn't believe it!

He Dipped Her Corn!

Then something astounding happens! Boaz invites her to come in and eat beside the *reapers* at his table.

(It was not customary that the gleaners would eat in the house with the reapers!) And **HE** passed the grain to her, as I say, "He dipped her corn!" The significance of this is eye-opening as we see his interest in this Moabite woman to whom he is showing such favor! He is personally taking care of her! (Remember he is Jesus, Ruth is the Church, or rather YOU and ME.) This is a picture of Jesus's love for us, and we see that His care for us knows no bounds. When she "rose up" to go back to glean, Boaz told his young men, "Let her glean, even among the sheaves...and let grain fall on purpose for her..."

I got so excited when I read this I could not sit in my seat! In today's language, let me tell you the prophetic word from this scripture: We are not only free to partake of the provision that has been left to us, but Jesus has given instruction that we can partake of ALL the field, not just a portion. It has ALL been given, and we can have as much as we want. God has dropped all provision in front of us, and our responsibility is only to *receive*. Most Christians I know just hang out in the corners of the field, hoping for a crumb. Reach out and receive what He has given you!

I have a message I call, "Come and Get It." The table has been set. The food is on the table. Everything, from meat and potatoes to every dessert known to man has been made available! Healing, prosperity, harmonious relationships are the heart of God for you, for all of us. Our only responsibility is to first "know" about these things, then go after them in faith, which many times is simply to "rest" in Him, and believe! Renewing our minds on the word of God is vital to our growth and witness. It is through meditating in the Bible that we "know" what we have already been given. If you don't know, you won't have.

Something else that is noteworthy here is that Ruth not only ate her lunch, but saved back a portion to take home to Naomi. Even in Ruth's being shown great favor, she did not forget her mother in law. As you and I are blessed so abundantly, let us not forget others who need the Lord and His grace.

Blessed Are You!
Chapter 3

Naomi had discovered by now that the wealthy land owner Ruth was gleaning from was a close relative, and she was more than a little excited! In chapter 2 when Ruth told her she had gleaned at the field of Boaz, Naomi exclaimed, "Blessed be he of the Lord, who has not forsaken his kindness to the living and the dead." I see her nearly jumping up and down, and clapping her hands!   For one thing, with the kinsman redeemer custom, Ruth would be taken care of from now on, and also Naomi would reap from the benefit of this "kinsman redeemer." I am sure a "mother-in-law" apartment is included!

In Chapter 3, Naomi tells Ruth straight up she is "seeking security" for her. Then she begins to give her instruction, which always amazes me every time I read this. Ruth used blind faith in obeying her sweet Naomi, not understanding the custom of these people. Naomi told her to go take a good bath, put on perfume, and dress in her best. She told her to go down to the threshing floor, where Boaz would be "winnowing the grain" that night. She was to hide herself until Boaz had finished eating and drinking. Then he would lie down. Ruth was instructed by Naomi to uncover his feet, then lie down there. Naomi said, "He will tell you what to do."

Ruth said she would do it. So, she went down to the threshing floor and did all Naomi had told her to do.

When he was winnowing the grain, he was using a bowl like tool to pitch the grain up into the air, and the wind would blow out the chaff and impurities. All that fell back into the bowl was the pure grain. Here the wind is the Holy Ghost, and it is He who blows out the chaff and impurities in us. Now, I know that we ARE pure, yes, we are *in our Spirits*. But our minds need the chaff blown out, and the only thing that can do this is the application of the Holy Ghost. The Spirit. The renewing of our minds by the word of God.

At midnight Boaz awoke and was startled as he saw the woman! "Who are you?" he asked. She told him who she was, and that he should "take her under his wing" because he is a close relative. ("Marry me.")

He said, "Blessed are you of the Lord, my daughter..." This indicates he was an older man. He told her that she had shown kindness by not going after the young men. As she represents the body of Christ today (you and me, the Church), we need to receive this instruction not to go after something different, more exciting, more lucrative, or appealing, but to stick with the Lord Jesus!

He told her not to fear, and that everybody in town knew she was a virtuous woman. Ruth is the only woman in the Bible called "virtuous" by name. He said there was a closer relative than himself. (He had already checked this out!) Boaz said to stay the night, and he would find out in the morning if the closer relative wanted to perform the duty of taking on Ruth as a wife and raising up a child.

"Don't let it be known that a woman came to the threshing floor," he said.

Can you imagine modern day CNN and MSNBC News? The Enquirer? It would have been quite a hullabaloo for the media. A man of great respect, honor, wealth and position is visited overnight by a woman from Moab!!! Oh, the shame!

Boaz filled her shawl with barley. God will fill whatever you will give Him to fill. And it will be more than enough. Boaz said he did not want her to go "empty-handed." God never wants us to be empty-handed either! Ruth gave the barley to Naomi. Naomi said Boaz would not rest until he had concluded the matter that day!

Kinsman Redeemer
Chapter 4

This chapter begins with Boaz going to the gate of the city and sitting down. Jesus has sat down at the right hand of the Father! I used to read in the Virtuous Woman portion (Proverbs 31:10-31) about the husband who sat at the city's gates among the elders of the land. I pictured this as him going to the doughnut shop and drinking coffee with the guys while his wife was out buying fields, dealing in real estate, sewing and cooking for her family and being the best wife on the planet. Can we laugh?

Truth is, this "sitting at the city's gate" indicates government. It is the place decisions were made for the city and the people. Boaz was well-respected, a wealthy land owner, and someone who was looked up to as a leader.

He said to the closer redeemer, "Come aside, friend, and sit down here." And he did. This in itself depicts the honor shown to Boaz. The man did not make excuses or say he did not have time. Then Boaz was able to get 10 more men to sit down! Twelve men sitting down. Twelve is God's number for organization and government.

When Boaz told the story, the man quickly said "I will redeem it." Then Boaz proceeded to say that on the day he purchased the property, he would also be responsible to raise up a child to "perpetuate the name of the dead."

Then the relative quickly said, "I cannot redeem it, lest I ruin my own inheritance." He already had a family and did not want to cause problems with another wife and more children. He said, "Buy it for yourself." Jesus bought the church with His own blood (see Acts 20:28). This is verse 8. New Beginnings. The world got a new beginning when Jesus paid the price for the Body of Christ, the church, and even the whole earth.

There were witnesses, and Boaz called them to confirm the transaction, and he claimed the kinsman redeemer rights. The witnesses began to prophesy. "The Lord make the woman who is coming to your house like Rachel and Leah, the two who built the house of Israel; and may you prosper in Ephrathah and be famous in Bethlehem."

Jesus in Every Book of the Bible

This makes me so excited! Prophesy of our Messiah way back then! Jesus is in every book of the Bible.

Boaz and Ruth were married, she had a son, and then the women began to prophesy to Naomi. "Blessed be the Lord who has not left you this day without a close relative; and may his name be famous in Israel. And may he be to you a restorer of life and a nourisher of your old age; for your daughter-in-law who loves you, who is better to you than seven sons, has borne him."

They (the neighbor women) gave him his name. They called him "Obed." Great grandfather of David, the Psalmist and King. Ruth and Naomi lived happily ever after. (As did Boaz.)

Obed means "servant / worshiper". Rahab was Obed's other grandmother. Her name means "spacious, broad, liberty".

When there is <u>intimacy</u> between us, (the church) and Jesus, our Husband, (we are already married), then there is reproduction! Fruit! And there is grace, freedom, and liberty, a broad space to dwell in. Let's look at Ephesians 5:28-32.

"So, husbands ought to love their own wives as their own bodies; he who loves his wife loves himself. For no one ever hated his own flesh, but nourishes and cherishes it, just as the Lord does the church. For we are members of His body, of His flesh, and of His bones. For this reason a man shall leave his father and mother and be joined to his wife, and the two shall become one flesh (Gen 2:24). This is a great mystery,

but I speak concerning Christ and the church."

This intimacy, by God's standards, can only come by marriage! We are already married to Jesus; He is already our Husband. We should be producing fruit if we are intimate. I believe the "Marriage Supper of the Lamb" is the wedding reception!

In Conclusion...

Because of Naomi's faith in following the leadership of God, Ruth, the Moabite woman, ends up in the direct lineage of the Lord Jesus Christ, and is one of the only 5 women named in the genealogies in the Gospel of Matthew. This passage in the first chapter of Matthew has neon flashing lights around it for me, because I have studied these women, and every one of them, though they were disadvantaged, got tremendous new beginnings from God! God has always provided grace for people.

In the book of Ruth, she is the Church. Boaz is Jesus. We have a new beginning, my friend, and this incredible love story shows us that anyone can enter the presence of the Lord, no matter what your background, where you came from, what family you are from; it does not matter. For Ruth, her favor from Boaz came because she had shown love and care for her mother-in-law. He noticed her; he had been told about her. (Let me say that you are being watched. There is someone who will notice your faithfulness, and could be your Boaz! Your life can turn around in one glance of a person who is willing and able to change your life.)

Also, it was the custom that a relative would marry a widow in the family so that a seed could come up from that family, so as to keep the lineage going. The baby, Obed, who was born to Ruth and Boaz was the great grandfather of David, who was the ancestor of Jesus. Boaz is known as the "Kinsman Redeemer", foreshadowing the redemptive power of our Lord Jesus Christ!

God wants us to see the importance of being faithful and obedient. Boaz said everybody in town knew Ruth was a "virtuous woman". She is the only woman in the word of God called "virtuous" by name. She was excellent. Loyal. All 85 verses are filled with revelation of this wonderful foreshadowing of our relationship as the Bride, the Church, with our Groom, Jesus! Eight is new beginnings, and the number five is God's number for "grace."

Nugget #4
THE MOTHER HEART OF GOD

I had a baby when I was 6 weeks away from my 40th birthday. When our daughter, Kami, was about 10 years old, she came down from her bedroom upstairs and said she had been praying, and God had spoken to her that I would have a baby by the time I was 40 years old. She had always wanted a baby sister or brother. We were surprised and also against this idea! Clifton and I told her, "Honey, you can't be saying 'God told me', when He didn't. She insisted, and would not relent! Finally, we told her not to say that anymore. A few people knew about it, but we didn't talk about it anymore.

Three or four years later we were in church camp (something we did every year for 16 years) and I was walking as I did every morning with my friend Donna. I made a statement to her that my monthly period was late, and I was never late. This was in July. She immediately started counting on her fingers. She said, "You will have the baby in March, you will be 40 in April, and Kami's prophesy is coming to pass!"

Whoa! What a deal. I soon began to be sick in the mornings, we went to our Doctor, and he confirmed our fears! After I cried, we decided we would be happy and go forward! It was a long nine months. I learned a lot! People would say to me, "I'm glad that's you and not me." And then there were the buttons at truck stops and gas stations, "I'd Rather Be 40 Than Pregnant."

Here I was, 40 and pregnant. The world had me "double cursed." Another one was, "Oh, you're having a late life baby." (With a pitiful tone and sad face.)

I soon started saying, "I'm glad it's me!" And the Lord began to send amazing prophesies to us about this baby. "He will be a restorer of Life to you, he is a baby born in due season, not a late life baby."

"This baby will be a singing evangelist. He will preach the gospel."

About three weeks before he was due, I had a condition called "vertigo", and I was violently vomiting and could not function. I was bedfast, only able to eat popsicles and very little food. I was constantly sick and because I was pregnant, I was not able to take any medication for the sickness. As I was just beginning to feel better, a week or so later, my water was leaking, so my doctor told me to go to the hospital.

It was March 16th, my mother's birthday, which made us very happy. BUT, alas, he was not coming so fast! Mom finally went home late at night, as I was not coming along like we had thought. Ultrasounds were not done as much as they are now, and my Doctor did not think it was necessary.

I was put in a room where a nurse was with me constantly. I did not know the danger the baby was in at the time. I was on oxygen, and I did hear the nurse tell the doctor on the phone that the baby's heart rate was descending.

I was not dilating very quickly. All night the nurse sat with me, and I had no idea about the concern they had for me and the baby. I had gone in to the hospital in the afternoon. The next day the doctor came in and said he wanted to do a C section. I said NO, I wanted to have the baby naturally. Finally, he said he was giving me an hour (to go from 4 to 10). If I did not have the baby in an hour, he would do a C section. Clifton and I started praying in tongues and my body kicked into gear!

It was rough! Cody had had a bowel movement inside the womb. I did not know that if he had swallowed a drop – ¼ teaspoon - of that fluid, it can be fatal, or cause serious problems for the baby. Also, the umbilical cord was tightly wrapped around his neck, which was the hold-up throughout the night. He couldn't get out! He says now that the devil tried to hang him before he could even be born!

At the moment of his birth, the doctor quickly unwrapped the cord, to reveal a purple baby! Clifton called him "Papa Smurf", the purple cartoon character, and he especially looked like the Smurf when they put the white hat on his little head! The other thing was, because I had so violently vomited, his head had been pounded on my pelvic bone to bruise his head. The whites of his eyes were blood red due to the cord being so tightly wrapped around his neck that the blood vessels burst in his little eyes.

And THEN, his bowels would not move! He had had a bowel movement in the womb, so we knew they worked, but 6 days went by with nothing. The doctor had him in a blue box used for the bilirubin. The hospital let me stay there, and they fed me, let me breast feed, and it was great to be right there. Finally, the doctor decided I needed to quit breastfeeding till Cody's little system was balanced out. It was a small hospital, so everyone knew we were all waiting for Cody to poop! The day it happened, it was broadcast all over the hospital, and we all rejoiced! The blue box was covered, top to bottom! He was naked in there, so as to let the light permeate as much of his skin as possible. We were allowed to go home that day.

We had three teenagers at the time. I had not had the other three "naturally", and I wanted to do that with this fourth and last child. Even though it had been a nightmare, I'm glad I did it. I would change a few things if I could go back. "Let's find out WHY the baby struggled all night to get out!"

Breastfeeding was also a top priority for this one. The red eyes healed up, as well as the bumps and bruising on his head.

About six weeks later, as I sat in my rocking chair early one morning, nursing my baby in front of our fireplace in the quietness of my Indiana country home, God's presence began to flow over me. This was when Cody was still a newborn, around the time of my birthday. Mother's Day was right around the corner. Something happened to me that morning. I did not ask for this. I was not praying, nor in a necessarily "spiritual" place in my mind, but God began to speak to me.

He said, "You know I am El Shaddai". We sang the song at church about El Shaddai, so I knew what it meant. "All Breasted One, Many Breasted One, More than Enough, God of Plenty". So, I thought to myself, "Yes, El Shaddai, All Breasted One." Then God blew my mind. He spoke to me. He said, "Just as you are nursing this baby, and he is receiving everything he needs from your breast milk, so I desire my children to nurse from Me, My breast is filled with everything they need."

He then directed me to Isaiah 66. That portion of my

bible was "crisp", telling me I had not dwelt over there, and had no idea what it said. I was amazed, simply mesmerized by what I began to read. This was 1988. I have grown in knowledge and revelation since then to understand that this chapter is speaking of the end of an era, and Israel, and the Church. But the word of God is relevant to what we need at the time we read or hear a teaching from the Bible. This portion of scripture was illuminated to me, and the Holy Spirit revealed some powerful truth to me that morning, and led me through a study that impacted my life.

Dynamic Revelation

Isaiah 66:9 asks a question:

"Shall I bring to the time of birth and not cause delivery? says the Lord. Shall I who cause delivery shut up the womb?" says your God."

The answer is, "Of course not!" Something that we need to look at here is, "Do you have a dream? Are you pregnant with a vision that you have been nurturing for years?

I want to encourage you that God will not let you down. He will deliver that dream. He will cause your vision to come to pass. If He put it in your heart, or "womb", He will bring it forth! Have hope in God, don't give up!

Verse 10:

"Rejoice with Jerusalem and be glad with her, all you who love her. Rejoice for joy with her, all you who mourn for her."

Here, the way I received it in 1988, Jerusalem is a type of the Church. I was reminded that the Church is us. (Believers) And also Jesus is the Head of the Church. I rejoice with the Church! What glory She will have when we begin to move in the heavenly power given to us! What Light will shine when we realize who we are in Him, and begin to flow in the love He has given to us to exemplify to the world! I believe we could shine right now if we could see who we are in Him. Some are beginning to shine! As I update in 2020, there is a great awakening coming across the earth! We belong to God, and He has plans for us to bring in the Harvest, being a reflector of His great love and faithfulness.

I have also mourned for the Church. I mourn for what people think of the Church because of all the pain we have endured due to faulty church leaders, or those individuals in the churches who have not represented Jesus as He should be represented. Even though I don't believe we are there yet, I can see more and more progress in believers coming to the forefront with the message of Grace and unconditional love. Cody has actually said, since he was a teenager, "Mom, the church has to change!" He had ideas, even back then; we could have learned from. Church is not to be boring! Our churches have always had a charismatic flare, and we have endeavored to keep it alive and on fire. (Not that every service has measured up!)

I saw God with a female side as He was speaking to me. Look at verse 11:

"That you may feed and be satisfied with the consolation of her bosom. That you may drink deeply and be delighted with the abundance of her glory."

In the King James Version of this scripture, it says "that you may *suck* and be satisfied..." Like a baby would suck at the breast of his momma, we are to "suck" or "feed" at the Breast of God, the All Breasted, Many Breasted One. We are to "drink deeply", not just sip enough to quench our thirst and then hop down from His lap. When we get up on the lap of God and partake of what He has provided for us, we are delighted, and we have abundance.

Consolation is "comfort". We are comforted by His presence and His substance. KJV says to "milk out" instead of "drink deeply" which I quoted above.

In I Thessalonians 2:7 the Apostle Paul said this:

"We were gentle among you, just as a nursing mother cherishes her own children."

There is an intimacy between a baby and his nursing mother! This is what God desires for us. A closeness, an intimacy.

I went to the encyclopedia to search out facts concerning the nursing mother. I found out that there are about 18 milk ducts which lead to the nipple where the milk is flowing to the baby. God immediately spoke to me about the 9 gifts and the 9 fruit of the spirit, representing the 18 tubes, or milk ducts. As we sit on the lap of the Mother-side of our Father God and "drink deeply" from His supply, and receive His comfort and abundance, we are going to have the fruit and gifts flowing through us. Those who move out in the power of God have been with Him intimately!

Another thing I saw was that in the first milk from the mother, the colostrum, are properties which boost the immune system of an infant. Those who partake of the milk from God's breast will be "immune" to the offenses which are sure to come. The more we nurse at the breast of God's love and compassion, the less offended we will be. I can tell you that I am not easily offended. Folks are always asking me if they have offended me, and I think, "What?" I tell them it is very difficult to offend me, but it can be done. (Smile) There is power in knowing God's love for us. In fact, I may say several times in this book that this revelation is the true life-changing fact that we all need more than anything else. God sent his Son to die on the cross and take upon Himself all our guilt, shame, and sin. His love for us in non-comprehendible with our natural minds. We must receive this by the Spirit.

Nursing at the breast of our Mother / Father God keeps us aware of His Presence and of His abounding love. When our minds are "stayed on the Lord", there is no opportunity to look elsewhere, and get sidetracked with what others are doing or thinking about us. Hence, no offense!

God has a female side. He is both male and female. I had never thought of this fact. It had never occurred to me. I was blessed above measure to be receiving such a powerful message that I knew God wanted me to share with my congregation, and my radio audience.

Just Like We Comfort Our Kids

This chapter in Isaiah continues with verses 12-13:

"Thus says the Lord; "Behold I will extend peace to her like a river, And the glory of the Gentiles like a flowing stream. Then you shall feed; On her sides you shall be carried, And be dandled on her knees.

As one whom his mother comforts, So I will comfort you; And you shall be comforted in Jerusalem."

It is truly difficult for me to express my elation, and

my utter amazement when I read this scripture and realized the impact it was having on me, and the impact I knew it would transmit to the people with whom I would share this. Do you see that GOD WILL CARRY YOU ON HIS HIP AND BOUNCE YOU UP AND DOWN ON HIS KNEE??? It is so dynamic to me that I carry a doll to give a visual to my groups when I teach on this subject. I carry the doll on my hip. I show them how personal – how intimate – God is with us, if we allow it. Just as we sit our babies and grand babies on our knee to comfort them and play with them, so God does that with us! Meditate on that for a minute!

The first part of this portion, verse 12, is equally powerful. Peace is extended to Jerusalem, a type of the Church, which is you and me. It is extended like a river. A river flows; a river has a majestic property attached to it. We will have peace flowing, a comfort and a calm should come over us as we meditate on the love God has for us as His very own.

In Conclusion

Verse 14 says that **when you see this**, "your heart will rejoice". Pray that you see God as your Mother, as well as your Father. The revelation here in these verses in Isaiah 66 is that God has everything we need made available. I was amazed that the thin breast milk was all Cody needed to grow, to flourish, to be nurtured. The milk from my breast was all he needed. The milk from the breast of God is all you need! When

Cody was a baby, my kids called him a "Titty Monster" because he seemed to want to nurse a lot. God said we need to be "Titty Monsters" for Him. Nurse as much as you want to. It is a place of safety and blessing. A place of comfort. Go to the lap of God and be refreshed and revived and renewed. Fill up on the love, the compassion, the gifts and the fruit, and then the purpose is that you share with everybody you can about what you have received.

I was blessed with a great grandson in 2015. As I was holding him as a newborn, he became hungry, and was starting to cry and was moving his legs and arms with discontent. I told Taylor, his momma – my granddaughter – "Here, he needs you."

As soon as baby Kase began to nurse, he calmed down, and when his little belly was full, he was completely limp, asleep, and at perfect peace! What a visual this example gives for us! And Cody was the same way, as God was teaching me this incredible truth.

Let God carry you on His hip when you need that. Allow Him to "dandle" you on His knee for comfort and strength, and rejoice in the closeness you share with your God!

I taught this in 1988 on the radio, and to my church on Mother's Day, then I put it up and honestly **forgot** all about it! In 1998, yes, 10 years later, a woman called me on the phone. We lived in Colorado Springs at the time. She was a radio listener from Indiana, and she asked me to come to her Ladies Meeting and share my revelation on Isaiah 66. I had no idea what she was talking about! She reminded me. I went, and I have taught this everywhere, all over the world, ever since! My CBC students absolutely loved it when I shared with them. Two worldwide ministries sent the message out as their "Tape of the Month." How could I forget something like this? Now I treasure it as one of my most powerful revelations. I hope you love it, too. Coming to an understanding of God's love for us is the greatest thing that can happen to any person.

Nugget #5

GRACE

It is only fitting to make Nugget #5 the Nugget on "Grace." Five is God's number for Grace.

My husband, after the healing of our marriage, started receiving revelation about the unconditional love of God. Andrew Wommack is the only minister we had ever heard preach this way. While I exceedingly admired Andrew and his teachings, there were some things he said that were hard for me to receive. I was a "works girl." I thought the reason I was so blessed was because I was the one who prayed for an hour, was highly disciplined in my worship, Bible reading, and being faithful. I thought that was why I was so blessed and received such favor from God. I had been self-righteous until the failed marriage and the way that my husband had planned to leave me. That will knock the wind right out of a girl's sails. All of my ritualistic prayer and discipline in the word had not produced my desired result. I had to start all over.

Clifton began to teach that all we have to do is believe in Jesus in order to go to Heaven and be blessed. "We already have all we need." Now remember this was

1985. NO ONE, and I mean NO ONE was teaching this where we lived, or in the sphere where we were involved in Southern Indiana.   Clifton preached "grace" when grace was not cool. (Remember "we were country when country wasn't cool"?) We started taking our preacher friends to Andrew Wommack's Minister's Conferences. He did not call them "marriage conferences" anymore after that first one. (His first Minister's Conference was a Marriage Teaching where Clifton and I began our restoration.)

The first message Clifton taught on the expanded grace message he was receiving from the Holy Spirit was a revelation from Matthew 7:13-14:

"Enter by the narrow gate; for wide is the gate, and broad is the way that leads to destruction, and there are many who go in by it. Because narrow is the gate and difficult is the way which leads to life, and there are few who find it."

Clifton's Vision

Clifton got a white board and drew on it to show the congregation what God had shown him this scripture means. He drew a big circle. Then he added a gate. It was narrow and straight. "Jesus IS THE GATE," he said. The teaching we had always heard and believed was, "You had better walk the straight and narrow, keep on the right path, or you are toast." No, that is wrong. All other ways out of the circle are wide and broad and they lead to destruction because they do not lead to Jesus. Jesus IS that straight and narrow way. He said, "I **AM** the way...." (emphasis mine)

Clifton then began to receive such radical revelation on God's love and grace that he thought he was a heretic, and would not preach it for a long time. When he did preach it – that we are not sinners – that God does not see us as sinners from the moment we receive Jesus as Savior and Lord, he got flak from other preachers, and from me. He preached this at the Lighthouse for 10 years with me coming in behind him teaching what all we needed to do to get our prayers answered and receive from God. I argued with him, I asked him question after question, "What about this or that, what about this scripture?" I was performing the formulas; he was flying high with freedom. He had answers, but I was still blind for 10 years!

One thing, though, that started the blinders coming off (for me) was I could not deny that even after my diligence for years of doing the "steps" and "formulas" I had learned in the circle I was in, I had come up empty concerning my marriage. Now, it **was** finally healed, but it was not because of any faith formula I exacted upon my situation. I had depended completely on the Holy Spirit speaking to me moment by moment. The steps did not work. And believe me, I "worked" them.

The Revelation

In 1995 we were sitting in a meeting at Dave Duell's church in Denver. We were spending the night with the Duell's because we were going up into the mountains to preach the next morning, and it was much closer from Denver than from Manitou Springs where we lived. Dave and Bonnie had their weekly service on Saturday night, and they had invited us to come to church and spend the night with them. We were attending their church at the time, after moving to Colorado.

In October of 1995 a guest speaker was ministering there at the church from the books of Romans and Hebrews on the subject of God's Amazing Grace. He stood in one spot with his Bible open in his hand, and delivered one of the most anointed messages we had ever heard. Something inside me broke. The word of God came in power and anointing. Clifton sat with tears streaming down his face. He said, "This man has said what I have known for years to be true, but was afraid or did not know how to say it." Basically, it was a simple message of the past being in the past, it is always a new day with God, and He is never holding anything against us as His children. Unconditional love on a plane above what we had heard before, or what had been revealed to us by the Spirit.

We were privileged to eat with him and the Duell's after church. We were ALL in a state of shock, and we asked him questions. He knew his stuff, and he calmly answered everything we asked. After he went to his hotel, we sat with Dave and Bonnie in their home till past midnight talking about this. Clifton and I went to our room, and the last time I looked at the clock it was after 4 am, and Clifton told me the next morning he was looking at the clock at 4 am also!

We could not sleep over this "too good to be true" gospel. The seed Clifton had planted in me for 10 years was finally full grown! In Conifer at the mountain church we told them everything we knew about all of the revelation we had received the night before concerning the unconditional love of God!

Grace In Action

God had tried to speak to me all along the way. One time we had gone back to Indiana to preach, and two of our family members needed jobs. One of them came to our church service on Sunday. He gave his tithes of what little money he had. He spent the day with us, and came back to church on Sunday night. We had prayed for him to get a job. He had applications in several places. On Monday morning he called us and excitedly said, "I got a job! I go to work tomorrow!" I said, "Oh, Praise the Lord, it is because you came to church, you gave money and prayed!"

Then the other family member came walking in the door. He had not gone to church. He gave nothing and did not pray. He had been out drinking Saturday night, and didn't wake up in time for church. He was so happy to report to us that he was hired for the same job as the other (holy) guy!

The Holy Ghost loves to get me! I said to the Lord, "What's the deal?" I did not understand this. It just goes to show you that God is God. He will have mercy on whom He will have mercy! The one who drank alcohol and did nothing for God that weekend had a calling on his life, and had been saved and filled with the Spirit at a young age. God is good. So much better than we can comprehend. God's grace is the only answer I ever got for my questions to God. Who knew if the drinker had prayed? Did God hear one prayer and not the other? I think He heard both prayers.

I am always receiving answers to prayers I don't deserve. I used to be so self-righteous. I used to be "able" to walk the straight and narrow, to pray, fast, worship, and do the steps. Then it all fell in on me. I found out "law" was not working for me any better than it did for the Pharisees. Give me Grace.

Divine Favor

Grace, in its simplest form, is (Hebrew #5485 from Strong's): *"divine influence upon the heart, and it's reflection in the life, including gratitude: acceptable, benefit, favor, gift, gracious, joy, liberality, pleasure.*

(Greek #2580, Strong's): *"kindness, favor, pleasant, precious, well favored."*

In one place it is *"beauty."* (James 1:11)

Under #2587 it is *"compassion."*

These are the Hebrew and Greek meanings for the word "grace". Some preachers try to make it something else. When we understand God's "grace" we begin to walk in the "favor" He has provided. The Apostle Paul greeted every church with "Grace and peace", and he signed off with grace, also.

Noah Found Grace

The first time grace is mentioned is in Genesis 6:8:

"But Noah found grace in the eyes of the Lord."

He found grace. How? I used to wonder. He actually had not done anything to deserve any grace. "Undeserved favor." His father had prophesied over him, though, "This one will comfort us concerning our work and the toil of our hands, because of the ground which the Lord has cursed." In the previous verses God said he was sorry he had made man, and was going to destroy him, "both man and beast."

God called Noah "righteous". Genesis 7. Righteousness is "right standing with God." My husband has written a good book called "Saint or Sinner?" It is subtitled, "How God Deals with the Sins of His Saints?" There are many more exhaustive and comprehensive teachings on this subject besides ours. For this Nugget book, I wanted to share a bit about how I came to the truth of the "Amazing Grace" appropriated by our Savior, and that He made a perfect work from the cross.

"Grace" is the meanings I have copied from the Strong's. Grace causes me to be able to continue in my call and not feel the condemnation I used to feel any time I did something wrong, or messed up, or even thought in a wrong way. There is so much condemnation brought upon us by the influence of the enemy and our own minds. God's amazing grace lets us continue to walk holy and righteous and blameless before Him. Ephesians Chapter 1 declares we have obtained an inheritance. We have redemption, forgiveness of sins, and we are sealed with the Holy Spirit of promise!

Complete in Him

In Colossians Chapter 2 we read in verse 10 that:

"...you are complete in Him...."

Complete. Whole. Strong's #4137 - "to fulfill, make full, to be filled, complete (often used with reference to the fulfillment of the Old Testament scriptures) fulfilled, ended, accomplished, make full, perfect."

This is what (who) we are! This is not who we are *striving to become*, as all of us are guilty of trying to do. This is who God has made us.

When we get a glimpse of God's divine, undeserved favor, we are changed forever. No more guilt, no more condemnation!

"There is therefore now no condemnation to those who are in Christ Jesus, who do not walk according to the flesh, but according to the Spirit." (Romans 8:1)

Are you in Christ Jesus? Are you born again? Do you believe? If your answers are "Yes," then you are perfect in the eyes of God. Not in your spouse's eyes, not in the eyes of any human being, but in the eyes of God. Yes, you are perfect, the apple of His eye, He carries your picture around Heaven! "See, here is my child!"

When we read "flesh" in Romans 8:1, most of us automatically think of some "fleshly, sinful deed." This is talking about walking in the flesh as in trying to do something to earn your salvation, or work for your ticket to "no condemnation."

If we are "walking according to the Spirit", we are living and walking in the realm of God's grace and favor. As we continue to read, in verse 8, Paul tells us that if we are in the "flesh", we cannot please God. It takes FAITH to believe we are righteous without doing the "right things." This is why "faith" was given. A measure was given to every man, because God knew it would take faith for us humans to believe we are righteous.

We are saved by grace. Undeserved, unmerited favor.

Waves and Moves

Sadly, just as every move of God seems to sweep in and be a great blessing, there are those who go off the deep end, taking the fresh revelation to places God never intended for it to go. In five decades of watching the trends and "waves" and assorted personalities ebb and flow – and crash and burn – I have somehow managed to keep in the flow of the Spirit. My husband and I never went off the deep end. We saw and sensed in our spirits when something was not right. I will talk about some of these "moves". Grace is NOT a "move" or "movement." Grace is the Gospel. The truth of God's word to humanity. One thing I thank my denominational church for was I learned that we are born again once and for all. "Once saved, always saved." God showed me this by the birth of my own children. They can't be "unborn." This is the reason God used the term, "born again." We as mothers know about birth! One can never go back into the womb.

After coming out of the denominational background, we had opportunity to fall into weirdness. The first "wave" we experienced was the Charismatic, Holy Ghost move of God which was authentic, anointed, much-needed, and widely received. This was a refreshing and a "come alive" experience! I studied the moves of God from the 20th century, and I realized He has been trying to tell us something for hundreds of years! A few answered the call, boldly, and presented the "new" revelation. New to them, not to God. I am talking about the Azuza Street Revival at the turn of the century. (1900's) I recommend that you read the book, Azuza Street by Frank Bartleman. A rich history has been recorded.

Reality of Freedom of the Spirit

Clifton and I and our church enjoyed the freedom of the Spirit, the healing, and other manifestations of the Spirit. We were certainly "accused" of being weird because we operated in the gifts of the Spirit. The Lighthouse was called "that church" by some townspeople. Smile. One of the abuses of this wave was that everybody and his brother claimed to be a "prophet." There was so much "prophesy" going around that it was uncomfortable, and much of it was erroneous. Men and women were telling each other, and people in the services, that "God said" things that maybe He did NOT say! It caused grief, and as a result of these off the wall "prophesies", folks were receiving and acting on the "words" and falling on their faces in failure.

It was difficult to watch, and if we tried to correct this, we were called "non-Spiritual." I personally held back on operating in the gift of prophesy during that time, because I had read in the Old Testament where false prophets were stoned! I believed my "words from God" must be exact and accurate. Later I realized that if we are moved upon to give a word of knowledge or wisdom or prophesy, we are only responsible to give what we hear, and not make a paragraph out of the "word." The person receiving has been prepared by the Holy Spirit. I learned that I don't have to understand the word, but my responsibility is to deliver the word!

The Prophetic Ministry is alive and vital to the body of Christ and to the world. There are prophets, and there are those who operate in the gift of the prophetic. We have ventured outside our "circle" for years now, to receive the prophetic ministry, the individuals who operate in this gift, and have opened up to be used also. I encourage others to move out and be used of God in this way!

Then there is the counterfeit. Or I could also say the "over-zealous" who want to be seen and recognized. They are not all "false prophets", but rather prideful saints trying to be "spiritual." It takes intimacy with the Father to know what to say and when to say it.

The Faith Message

The Faith Message put the spotlight on the Word of God, which was desperately needed at that time. (It is needed ALL the time!) Clifton and I were so excited to hear these things, and try the word, and see that it really worked! We were fanatical, which is not all wrong, but the way we were perceived by our people (congregation) was wrong. Never meaning to, we left them feeling "less" because maybe they could not rise to the level of faith they thought they saw in us.   We went overboard. No medicine. Why use medicine if God is the Healer? Not even aspirin or vitamins. For about 10 years! No doctors, no insurance. No Band-Aids. Raising three kids. I thank God for the day we saw that the "formulas" do not work. Only a relationship with the living Spirit of God – Our Loving Father – will work. The formulas and "steps" failed me.   God never failed me. Love never fails.   He brought me out to a better way of flowing in the Spirit and living for Him, trusting Him every day. Grace.

More on the Prophetic

The Prophetic move of God came about the same time as the "Word of Faith" was popular. Somehow there seemed to be a rift between the two. The prophets and the faith people did not fellowship. Finally, thank GOD, everyone who was listening to the Spirit saw the need for BOTH. Clifton and I lived in the boondocks. Our church was located miles from town in the midst of corn fields and cow pastures, and we were shielded from a lot of foolishness. For years we had very little fellowship. We went through the "School of Hard Knocks" and "Burning Bush University." We graduated with excellent grades and honors. (Smile) We never did hold famous teachers in such high esteem that we worshipped them. (Except in the beginning, I would have to say we did "worship" the "Faith Teachers".) After we saw that formulas do not work, we developed a relationship with the Spirit of God, who always leads in love.

Then Came Grace

Then came Grace... Amazing Grace! Andrew Wommack shared the message of "Grace and Faith," and brought it all into perspective for us. Then we had to receive the revelation for ourselves. Hearing a teaching is one thing, receiving the revelation is another. I have shared in my "Rose" book our testimony of our receiving the grace revelation. We don't have it "all", we are still learning. But we do understand the unconditional love of God and that He loved us before we were ever born, and that He has a plan, and we are no longer under the penalty of sin! We have learned that God is not judgmental, and He wants us to love people where they are, like He loves us – just where we are. He is not on a pilgrimage to "change" us. However, we cannot help but change when we receive the revelation of His Great Love!

What Grace Isn't

Here's what Grace is **NOT**: A license to sin. You have all heard that one. "Grace is just a license to sin." As my husband and many others say, "No one needs a license, we were all doing pretty well at sinning without a license."

Jesus paid the penalty for our sin. We no longer are under that penalty of breaking the "laws". And God's love remains.

Something those say who have no understanding: "Do you mean to tell me I can go kill somebody or rob a bank and God will not do anything about it?" First sign of "NO understanding!" Would you rob a bank now? Would you kill somebody now? Then why would you do it just because you find out you are under grace?

The other thing is some who think they understand Grace start drinking to excess, stop giving to the church, stop going to church, and get into a proverbial ditch. I believe the truth is, they start doing what they always wanted to do anyway, but were in fear of what God would do to them. Freedom was not free, it cost the blood of our Savior. And Freedom comes with responsibility. I know someone who got into adultery and "said" he thought it was okay because of his perception of "grace." It is not okay! He said that he was under grace, but somehow, I don't believe he TRULY believed that it was okay to become an adulterer and leave his wife and family. See how messed up people are? And simultaneously God's love pours upon this individual. So, you are asking, "What, then?" It is simple. Number one, it's not over. Judge not. "Judge nothing before the time...." the Apostle Paul said. Also, he will reap what he is sowing. This is a spiritual law from Genesis on through the Bible. Whatever we sow, we will reap. Time is a factor. And God still loves him as if he was pure, holy, and righteous. The human part of us rebels. His wife rebels! Thank God he has a place to go (God) when he comes to himself.

Grace to Serve, not Sin

Then there are many who still believe they can go to hell for committing a sin. Then why would Jesus have to give His Life? If we can get to Heaven by our works, who needs Jesus? That is oversimplifying, but you get the point. Our sin was paid for – in full - once and for all. Understanding what God has done for us by giving grace and unconditional love should motivate us to get MORE involved, not less! It is NOT Grace to go into a sinful lifestyle just because you find out God is not mad at you!! The Bible is still the Bible! God's holy word! He has given us grace so we can serve, not so we can sin.

"Grace" is not "inclusionism", nor is it "universalism". These cults say that there is no hell, and everyone is saved whether they want to be or not. Some will argue, but the Bible is clear that we **do** have a choice to make as to whether we want God or not. Our call is to represent God and His love in such a manner that others will want to know Him. And "Yes, Virginia, there really is a hell." We don't talk about it often, because we like to talk about Heaven. It's like when you are going on a vacation to Florida, you aren't telling everyone about Alaska! Jesus made it clear there is a hell. It is for those who reject of the Son of God. The only ones who go to hell are those in unbelief and rejection.

God's Love

We who have a little knowledge of grace know that Jesus's whole trip to earth was to provide a way for us to see Grace, and a way for us to see God clearly. It was to show us what Love looks like, what God is truly like. We as humans, at our very best, come up short on understanding concerning God's love for us. I have said for years, and will probably say again in this book: "If we knew how much God truly loves us, it would change our lives." We would no longer be insecure, jealous, sick, or in lack. His love is pure liquid courage and confidence, for lack of better words. I am not talking about a "self-confidence", but a "knowing" that God is going to take care of us. I am growing in this. I am a lot closer than I used to be. As Andrew Wommack says, "I have not arrived, but praise God, I've left."

The best thing about this is, it is NOT HARD, it is not at all difficult when we find that intimate place in HIM. How do we do that? The Bible says when we seek Him with all our hearts, we will find Him. It also says those who are not even seeking Him will be found of Him! So, do we seek, or do we let Him find us? I have always thought – because of the way I have received revelation from the word – that He seeks us our whole life until we become "apprehended by Him", then it is our place to pursue Him to find out what all He has given us in our inheritance. We are rich beyond measure!

Great Nugget here...

God knows your heart. He knows what you need and want before you pray. There is a river to flow in where you just rest and live your life in the realm of the spirit, and of the love of your Father. The Message Bible calls it the "unforced rhythms of grace." Most people try too hard. Jesus said his yoke is "easy" (see Matthew 11:28-30).

Grace Means Freedom

Grace means FREEDOM. It was for freedom Christ has set us free! We don't toil to get into grace! Grace is a place of REST. Receiving "undeserved favor" causes rest. Knowing He is going to take care of us produces rest and peace. Faith is involved. If we don't believe this grace is available and we pass it by, there is no faith involved to receive. Without faith it is impossible.

God has made it simple. Preachers make it hard. Churches, religion make it seem we can never arrive or attain. We are taught we must always be striving not to sin, not to even have a bad thought. Altars are full every Sunday with well-meaning believers on their knees confessing and repenting and crying their eyes out over their behavior they believe to be sins. What does this do to help the person? Nothing. It only leaves a "sin consciousness", which is what God is trying to rid us of, and He did it by sending Jesus to cleanse us from ALL unrighteousness.

Grace – the overwhelming sense of a heart that has believed God for who He is, who He has made you, and for what He said He would do for His children. You really are the "apple of His eye", and the object of His affection. Let this soak in your spirit, and renew your mind to the revelation that God loves you. I John 4:10, "*In this is love, not that we loved God, but that He loved us, and sent His Son to be the propitiation for our sins.*" Propitiation (Strong's #2435) "Atoning sacrifice, the means of forgiveness."

Our "identity" is in Christ Jesus now. We identify with Him. We are "in Him". There are many scriptures which talk about our place "in Him." When God looks at us, He sees us IN JESUS!

Nuggets on Grace from the Old Testament

Many New Testament writers brought sayings from King ~ Psalmist David over to describe certain truths not to be locked away in the Old Covenant. These are valuable for us as we read them and incorporate them into our lives.

King David Found Grace

We think of Grace only coming in with Jesus, but just as I gave the example of Noah, who "found grace" in the eyes of the Lord, King David also received grace and mercy in his time of deep sorrow.

David was the "apple of God's eye," the scriptures tell us. He was a man "after God's own heart". And yet his human-ness broke through to commit not only adultery, but also murder. After he brought Bathsheba to his house for a night of passion, (his idea, not hers) and she became pregnant, he then began a plot to deceive her husband into thinking it was his baby. David brought Uriah home from the war, and pretended to see how things were going, inquired about the leadership and the people, and sent him home to have a night with his wife. He also sent a gift of food to them, a gift from the King.

Uriah had more integrity than David did, as he refused to sleep with Bathsheba, knowing the other troops were on the battle field in distressful circumstances.

He could not enjoy himself in the arms of his wife, knowing that his comrades were suffering. He instead slept at the door of the King's house. Then the King brought him to supper and got him drunk, hoping that would send him to Bathsheba, but, again, Uriah would not succumb to these temptations out of loyalty to the King and his fellow servants, soldiers. David then sent a note *by* **Uriah** to Joab, the Captain of the army, saying, "*Put Uriah in the front line of the heaviest fighting, and withdraw from him, that he may be struck down and die.*" (II Samuel 11:15, AMP)

This story is deep and wide with theology and revelations, and it is a matter to be taken up at a time when an entire message can be prepared. For my "nugget" teaching, I will simply show that David did receive a new beginning and amazing grace from God. That is not to say there were not consequences to his actions. There were. David suffered tremendous grief and pain and some of the Psalms reveal just how near death he was because of what he did. In Psalm 51:1 he was praying, "H*ave mercy upon me, O God, according to Your steadfast love; according to the multitude of Your tender mercies and loving-kindness, blot out my transgressions.*" In verses 10-12 he stated, "*Create in me a clean heart, O God; and renew a right spirit within me. Cast me not away from Your presence, and take not Your Holy Spirit from me. Restore to me the joy of Your salvation, and uphold me with a willing spirit.*"

Of course, we know that "today" this is never a prayer we need to pray, because God has promised He will never leave us nor forsake us, and that his gifts are without repentance, in other words, He will never take anything from us He has given. He will never cast us away from His presence as a new covenant believer!

David "Got It"

David, the King, the Prophet, the Psalmist got it! He understood. He believed and spoke of his deliverance. In Psalm 52 he writes these words in verses 8-9: "*I am like a green olive tree in the house of God; I trust and confidently rely on the loving-kindness and the mercy of God for ever and ever. I will thank You and confide in You forever, because you have delivered me and kept me safe...*"

I am amazed at the depth of David's praise and his knowledge of the love of God, knowing that he did not possess the Holy Spirit as we do today, since Jesus was raised from the dead, and descended again on the Day of Pentecost in the Person of the Holy Spirit. The Spirit "came upon" the prophets in the Old Testament. We today have the Spirit of the Living God on the inside of us, living and dwelling and abiding there! What joy this evokes!

David's new beginning, because of God's mercy and grace, was enjoyed by him for the rest of his life. His family suffered from his betrayal, and he had to live with that. However, he served and praised and reigned. His story has inspired others throughout the centuries to repent and start all over, to take advantage of the grace offered by the King of the Universe, the Author of Salvation. It is free, and it is for all. Our part is to believe it is true.

Nugget #6
EMERGENCY? CALL 911!

I was at home one weekend while Clifton was out of the country preaching. Someone came back our lane – we lived ¼ mile back a narrow gravel lane, surrounded by fields and woods – off of a state highway. Ours was the only house back there. The man was asking directions to somewhere. He seemed a little "off", but got his directions and walked back out towards the highway. I did not think about it anymore during the day that Saturday.

That evening I was reading my Bible, getting ready to minister on Sunday in Clifton's absence. My daughter Kami was 14, and she was spending the night with a friend, so the only ones at home were me and my infant, Cody.

At about 10 o'clock I heard a noise outside. Our Pit Bulldog "Pig" did not make a sound, so I was a bit afraid. I have never been scared to stay by myself, but since the strange man had come to my house that afternoon, my mind started going crazy. We were so far off the beaten path that we did not even get Trick or Treaters, and in 18 years of living there, we only had one Jehovah's Witness!

I thought, "This man has killed my dog, and now he is going to kill me and my baby." There was no such thing as locks on our doors, or if there were, we had no keys. I put a chair up under the door handle in the family room where I was studying. Then I got Clifton's shotgun, which I had never used, nor did I know how to shoot any gun. "Does it have shells?", I wondered. I thought the potential thief, murderer, rapist would see I had a gun and leave. Lots of windows.

I then called Kelly, my son, who lived a few miles from us, and I asked him to come and check on things. After a little while I saw headlights in my driveway, and expected Kelly to come to the door, but after a while, the vehicle backed out of the driveway and left. I thought, "Ok, things are fine, Kelly has inspected the outside."

"Call 911"

While I was waiting for Kelly, the Lord began to speak to me, "Call 911." I knew it had to be a spiritual 911, because there was no 911 service in our area in 1989. The only way I knew about 911 was hearing about it on TV.

As I was looking in the Bible, trying to find a 911 scripture to see what God was trying to tell me, the Holy Spirit took me to Psalm 91:1. I started reading, and a peaceful calm came over me.

(KJV) "He that dwelleth in the secret place of the Most High shall abide under the shadow of the Almighty."

I meditated on that scripture, and saw the protection I had in God if I would just "abide" in His presence. The "shadow" is "protection, shade." (Strong's Exhaustive Concordance #6738) Then as I continued to read, verse two says: "He is my refuge and my fortress." There are several verses in Psalm 91 that speak of the fact that we are not to be afraid. Verse 5 (God's number for Grace) tells us, *"Thou shall not be afraid..."* Verse 10: *"There shall no evil befall thee, neither shall any plague come nigh thy dwelling."*

Then the Psalmist went ahead to encourage me in the fact that the angels have charge over me to *"keep thee in all thy ways."* I was being protected by angels! This became a revelation to me!

In verse 14, David shifted gears and this Psalm is now **God** speaking through David about us! He became prophetic!

"Because he hath set his love upon Me, therefore I will deliver him: I will set him on high, because he has known My name. He shall call upon me, and I will answer him; I will be with him in trouble; I will deliver him and honor him. With long life I will satisfy him, and show him my salvation."

After I received this message, I went to bed. Peaceful and calm.

Kelly Didn't Come!

The next day at church I thanked Kelly for coming over so late to check on me, and he had a look on his face like, "What?" He had not come! There was no gas station open that late the night before, and his truck gas gauge said empty. There was no small stir in my heart as I thought, "Who was that in my driveway at midnight?" That mystery was never solved.

My students at CBC (Charis Bible College) had me a plaque made with the inscription **"Emergency? Call 911".** They never forgot that teaching, and they bring it up to me to this day. I have not forgotten it either! We need not fear. Call 911.... go to Psalm 91:1 and practice dwelling under the safety of God's sheltering wings.

Nugget # 7
SHADRACH, MESHACH, AND ABEDNEGO

This is just a short revelation which is intriguing and powerful. I did hear this from another minister in 1984. It hit me like a ton of bricks, or like a wildfire, and I have never forgotten it. I have mentioned it several times in my teachings over the years. I have never heard it from anyone since our friend Slim Thompson preached on the book of Daniel at our church in 1984. The way it has always been preached is the three boys said if they got thrown into the fire, they still would not serve the tin god. Well, no, because they would be dead. But think about this:

This story is in Daniel Chapter 3. The story is about the three Hebrews who were threatened by King Nebuchadnezzar, and were told they would be thrown into the fire if they did not bow to the image that the king had set up. Most everyone has heard this story.

In verse 17 (KJV) they said *(Italics, **BOLD CAPS, and parentheses** are mine):*

"IF IT BE SO, *(that you throw us into the fire)* our God whom we serve is able to deliver us from the burning, fiery furnace, and He will deliver us out of thine hand O king. **BUT IF NOT** *(if you do not throw us in)* be it known unto thee O king that we will not serve thy gods, nor worship the golden image which thou hast set up."

It had never made sense to me that they would say, "Well, if God does not deliver us, we won't serve" .... they never said that!! That is how it has been taught for years, and when I heard this revelation, it was like "whoosh", down into my spirit, and it made sense then. "If you throw us in, **God will deliver us**, if you don't throw us in, we still will not serve your tin god." I love it! They had faith and knew God would deliver them! They did not say, immediately after they said He would, that He might not.

A cool thing is, the KING, Nebuchadnezzar, "blessed the God of Shadrach, Meshach, and Abednego" and said there was no other God who could deliver in this way! THEN, later in chapter 6 when Daniel was about to be thrown to the lions, the king said to him, "Your God will deliver you!"

People notice when God does things for you, and they know where to go when they need a miracle. And, of course, as you read this you see that God shut the mouths of the lions, and in the morning, Daniel was unharmed!

I hope the insight about the three "Hebrew Children" was an "ah ha moment" for you like it was for me.

How does this apply to us today? In the world we live in, Christians are faced with more persecution than ever in my lifetime. You might be guessing that it is only just beginning. "Hate speech" is no longer what it used to be, but now it is considered hate speech if we talk about Jesus or the Bible.

Christians all over the world are persecuted, and being killed for their faith. I learned when I was in the Middle East, that there is a genocide against Christians.

What will you do if confronted with "Reject Jesus or die"? God will keep us alive until we have fulfilled our destinies as long as we follow Him and listen.

I want to be like Shadrach, Meshach, and Abednego! I want to stand fast and declare the deliverance of our God!

Nugget #8
THE TEACHER

A revelation that my husband shares is so profound and yet so simple, and he tells a funny story with it. The Holy Spirit is described as our Teacher in the Word. When we realize this, and give Him place, life becomes easier. Clifton puts himself down for not always using the correct English when speaking, but he says if he carried his high school English teacher around in his chest, he would never have to worry. Edna Teaford ("Old Maid" school teacher, never married) was his dad's English teacher, and his, and mine. She requested to be called "MISS" Teaford.

She had the 10th grade English book memorized! So, we DO have the Holy Ghost living inside of us, and are without excuse not to know what's going on!

There was a young man who had moved to our school from Kentucky. One day in English class Miss Teaford announced there would be a test, and for the students to get out their paper and pencils.

We will call him Robert. Where he was from, the students stood to address the teacher. So, Robert stood and said, "MRS. Teaford…"

And before he could ask his question, or make his statement, Miss Teaford said, "Ohhh, Robert, Ohhh Robert, it's MISS Teaford, MISS Teaford, not MRS!"

Robert: "Miss Teaford, (dragging out each word with a Southern drawl) I hain't got nary pencil."

Ohhhhh, Robert, Oh Robert, Not hain't got nary!"

Robert: "Hain't got no?

And the strait-laced, very prim and proper and all business English teacher lost it and laughed! Then everyone laughed!

The point being, if only Robert had had Miss Teaford coaching him from the inside, he would have had no trouble. We have THE TEACHER residing within us!

We, as believers, have the Holy Spirit, this incredible gift – this all-knowing Being living in us – to warn us of things to come, to help us in our infirmities, to help us pray as we ought, and to give us the gifts of the Spirit when needed. We have THE TEACHER at our disposal at all times. All we have to do is access the knowledge and wisdom by recognizing the Holy One we possess.

Nugget #9
WORSHIP

I noticed something one day as I was preparing for a bible study, I was doing on Tuesday mornings. My subject was going to be on the different words for worship, and the multiple ways there are to execute "worship." It was going to be about the different words translated "worship" from the Bible. However, my teaching transformed from those words for Praise and Worship into what I saw worship producing! Right away I saw that Abraham was taking Isaac to the mountain to sacrifice him, as the Lord had asked him to do (see Genesis 22).

Abraham did not question God. He heard his instruction. He got up early in the morning and took two young men, Isaac, and the wood for the burnt offering. On the third day he saw the place afar off. He told the two young men, "*Abide ye here with the ass; and I and the lad will go yonder and worship, and come again to you.*"

Isaac asked, "Where is the lamb for the burnt offering?"

Abraham said, "God will provide himself a lamb for the burnt offering."

We all know the story. There had been a ram coming up the other side of the mountain during the time Abraham was climbing the mountain to offer Isaac. The ram got caught in a thicket, and was available at the moment Abraham needed him! An angel appeared and advised Abraham of the present circumstance. He no longer had to sacrifice his son, but a substitute had been provided. I call this a miracle. Just "natural" for God, but a miracle to us.

Abraham offered the ram instead of his son. This caused a chain reaction we enjoy to this very day. We are Abraham's "seed". We possess the gates of our enemies (see Genesis 22).

In Exodus 24 God told Moses to come up and worship and to bring Aaron, Nadab, Abihu, and seventy of the elders with him. This portion of scripture was pointed out to me after I had read the bible multiple times, served the Lord for 40 years, and had been in full-time ministry most of that time. I was in a seminar with Mary Dorian, and she nonchalantly waved her hand and said, as a side note, that Moses and 73 others had had a meal with God. I had never before done this, but I raised my hand in the meeting and asked where this was located in the bible! She just calmly said she'd find it later and continued with her session on dreams and visions. As the day went on, I forgot about it, and did not get the scripture. When I got home, I was telling Clifton about it, and he had not remembered such a thing, either, but I had my bible in my lap, and I said, "Well, it has to be in the front part!"

I am seriously telling you my bible fell open to Exodus 24! My eyes went immediately on the very scripture I wanted to find! As I read this, I was astounded and amazed.

Verses 9 – 11 (KJV)

"Then went up Moses, Aaron, Nadab, and Abihu, and seventy of the elders of Israel: And they saw the God of Israel: and there was under his feet as it were a paved work of a sapphire stone, and as it were the body of heaven in (his) clearness.

And upon the nobles of the children of Israel he laid not his hand: also, they saw God, and did eat and drink." "He laid not His hand" means He did not kill them!

PEOPLE!!!! This happened when? After they were called to WORSHIP! Let me expound just a minute on these verses.

My whole point is that miracles happen after we have worshipped! But I want to say that this chapter in Exodus sent me on a study that I am still pursuing 9 years later.

I began to ask ALL of our preacher friends, young and older than I was, if they knew this. NO ONE remembered ever seeing this in the word of God. NOT ONE, and I knew dozens well enough to ask.

One thing that blew me out of the water is, if this happened THEN, why couldn't it happen NOW? My answer is, it could, and it does!

As I am finishing this book in May 2020, there are unprecedented happenings on the earth both in the natural realm (Coronavirus) and in the Spiritual realm.

I listen to a few modern-day prophets. I listen to the ones who bear witness with what the Holy Spirit is showing me, personally. Although I have not operated very much in the prophetic, I know I have that gift from the beginning of my Holy Ghost days. God gives me visions when I lay my hands on the saints for prayer. Sometimes I tell them what I see, sometimes not.

I am looking for a good outcome in this tragic, unbelievable mess! ("The Virus") My teaching to my church and to those who follow me is that, first of all, we face and defeat FEAR! I am convinced that the media perpetrates fear in such a powerful way, that without the word of God, we are crushed by it. Of course, Psalm 91 has been used, and rightfully so, but for me, even more is the revelation of God's love and care for His children! One man said 2020 is a year, and for four years, we will have the burdens lifted. I do believe that we will experience VICTORY! The last Harvest will include all those we have looked at with disdain with their tattoos, piercings, wild clothing and hair. With Cody's Love Movement group coming to our church this has started for us! Our people are so loving and accepting, and give them a warm welcome! They are hearing the LOVE OF GOD preached and are transforming before our eyes!

WORSHIP is a huge key! They love our singing and the effect it has on them. God's Spirit is tangibly present, and He moves like a river throughout the house, touching people, drawing them to Himself.

I don't mean to look at worship as a "work" or a magic formula. However, when we walk in a realm of continual worship, or recognizing God as our Savior, our Lord, our Everything, miracles happen. Amen!

Nugget #10
FINANCES

This nugget on finances is vital to our lives. God had a lot to say about our money. To get into debt is a binding force. We have been debt free, and we have been so deeply in debt that we were feeling like there was no hope. Being debt free is better!

There is plenty of scripture to help us in any area of life, and money is no different. We have been given the keys to prosperity. Look at III John 2:

"Beloved, I pray that you may prosper in all things, and be in health, just as your soul prospers."

Knowing it is God's will for us to prosper in all things is enough for us to be excited about prosperity. KJV says *"Beloved, I wish **above all things**...."* That is strong. Above all things, I want you to prosper and be in health, just as your soul prospers. Our soul is our mind, will, and emotions. I have a nugget on getting the word of God from our heart into our minds. It comes by renewing our minds on the word of God. When we know what He has said, and we believe Him, then our lives will change forever! I can remember before I knew the word of God, newly married, a new mother, and our finances were low, all I knew to do was worry.

Deposit, Withdraw

After I became a Spirit-filled Christian, I began to see that there is another Plan besides the world's plan. GOD HAS A PLAN! He has all the treasure we will ever need, and it is available to us. We make deposits, and we withdraw. In the Heavenly Kingdom, it is the same way. There is a myriad of teachings in the bookstores and on CDs on how to manage your money. There are TV preachers who will tell you if you give to them, you will have a home paid off, or become debt free in X amount of time. I am not against these men of God, but certainly one must be discerning! Giving to God has been reduced to people thinking they are being ripped off. I have come to the place of: "I don't care what other people do, or how it seems there is greed in the body of Christ, I will give my money to God, and He will see that it goes to the right place."

Giving does bring abundance into your life. The motive behind the giving is really the issue. Why do we give? When it is out of gratefulness, this is wonderful. If it is out of love, great! Obedience? Good reason to give. To "give to get" is not the best motive, yet we know a farmer definitely sows with a harvest in mind! So, I am saying there is a time to "give to get." If you need money, sow some money into a good ministry, into a man of God's life, or into a church.

Proverbs 3:9-10

"Honor the Lord with your possessions,
And with the first fruits of all your increase;
So your barns will be filled with plenty,
And your vats will overflow with new wine."

Hot Topic

This isn't just a nice verse. Remember that as a
Proverb, it was written by the wisest man who ever
lived! He is giving some 21st century instruction here.
"Honor the Lord." The "first fruits" here is also
descriptive of the "tithe." I know this word puts a lot
of grace people in the fetal position, but nevertheless,
the first fruits and the tithe as a gift to the Lord are as
"now" as any salvation message or message on grace.
Something that is tried and true is an anchor. For my
husband and me, tithing has been a practice we have
kept since we first heard it taught in the Baptist church
on the second Sunday after we were saved. Giving
10% of your money to God is just a simple way to
start with giving. To write a check for exactly the
amount of your tithe and stop there is "law." You are
under a law you made for yourself if that is the way
you give. This subject of "giving" is a hot topic, and
I am probably in the minority as to my perception, and
the way I see the word on it. It seems to me we can
give our way out of almost anything. But it is a heart

issue. What is in your heart? Clifton and I have always wanted to give from our hearts. We tithed when we did not have enough money to pay our bills, yet our bills were always paid. We have given mostly out of LOVE, which goes beyond a simple 10%. There are three levels of giving: Give because it is required, give because there is a need, and give because you love God and people, and it is in your heart to do it.

Jesus spoke much on money. I recommend Robert Morris's "The Blessed Life" series. For my "nugget" here, I want to say that I know many folks who have more money than they know what to do with, but still are not happy. The love of money is the root of all evil. Loving money will prevent one from giving it away, yet giving away money can open the door to give that person something that money can never buy. The big revelation here is: Do what the Lord is speaking to you to do. Then you can never go wrong! And remember, you really "can't take it with you"!

Folks are concerned about "investing" their money so it will grow over a period of time, and they will have more. Clifton and I have the testimony that our "investment" for all our ministry lives has been into the gospel. We have sold everything loose to put into the church, or our traveling ministry. We do not regret it, although at our ages now, while most people are retired, we are still full force in following the leadership of God to "go".

And if God does not send in the finances for us to live and go forward, we are in trouble!

Money and Ministry: I recently heard of a woman minister who was "hired" to come and teach a session in a conference nearby. I was surprised above measure to hear what she was charging as a fee to come and minister the word of God. Since she was charging such an exorbitant amount of money, I'm sure she didn't have to worry about her bills. That is the attitude of a "circle" of preachers we have never experienced. God has always taken care of us, and spoken to the saints to sow into our ministry, and sometimes our personal lives. Our preacher friends all come at our invitation, as they hear from the Spirit to come, not "charging" a dime, but trusting that their needs will be supplied. It only takes one person obeying God to meet all the needs. The ideal situation is for EVERYBODY to give as they are led of the Spirit. That does not normally happen. Why not?

Fear

I am convinced that fear is at the root of why the saints do not give freely, and why they do not step out and do what God is directing them to do, in any area. Fear of "not having enough" if they give, even though they sense the Lord is directing them to give a large gift. I understand the thinking, but it is wrong! My husband is exceedingly generous. I was taught from my youth to be frugal with money. I was delivered from the fear of letting go of money. We have a view that is not widely accepted, but we give abundantly when we have it, or when we do not have it. We believe that the reason we always have what is needed at the time is because we trust God. We believe His word. There is a lot of information on finances in the gospels, taught by Jesus.

Paul told the Philippians that because they gave to his ministry, all their needs would be supplied. Chapter 4 in the letter to the Philippians there is sandwiched in a truth, a nugget, that is meaningful. First, they gave to Paul, then he told them, "*...my God shall supply all your need according to His riches in glory by Christ Jesus.*"

Notice Paul said God would supply all YOUR need. Most people who quote this scripture say "all MY need." "God will supply all MY need". Paul said God would supply all YOUR need. Let that soak in, it is important! When we make it about others instead of ourselves, there is power in that.

"*My heart overflows with joy when I think of how you showed your love to me by your financial support of my ministry.*" Philippians 4:10 (TPB)

He also said here in this chapter that he knew how to be in lack, and he knew how to "experience overwhelming abundance". Yes, we identify with this statement!

Listen, finances are something the enemy uses to stop the word from going forth into the nations. Clifton and I have always pushed forward, money or no money. We have used credit cards, and we have been free of credit. We have been so deeply in debt we did not think we could breathe. We have also had all debt paid. We have had excellent credit, and we have had bad credit. Even though I think of ourselves as having integrity in all areas, I'm sure others would question that statement if they examined our credit report. At our age now I want to leave the earth debt free! I believe God is doing it!

The Bible says that the "*wealth of the wicked is laid up for the just.*" (Proverbs 13:22) Have you ever wondered how this would transpire? It did not seem right that God would just rip money away from people! What if we as believers are going to GET THE WICKED SAVED???? Then the finances would come rolling in! This is just an idea, but a good one. We led a guy to the Lord early in our ministry who owned a tavern. He was transformed and soon sold his tavern, bringing his tithe to us!

Clifton heard God say one time, "Jesus went to the poor, and the rich came to him." We went to the poor in a big way. In the middle of that, a rich man showed up in our service. He was enamored with the way we had church, and the things we said. He gave us church property worth about a million dollars or more.

The first part of that scripture says this: "*A good man leaves an inheritance to his children's children...*" Inheritance is more than money, but includes money.

This used to bother me, and I felt guilty, thinking there may not be any inheritance, since we spent all and used all for the gospel. Then the Lord spoke to me one day and said I had left an inheritance worth more than gold to my children and their children by the word that was sown and exemplified to them. I do believe to leave them wealth also.

In closing, "finances" is a subject we can discuss all day. I am rich. Not in money, my bank account is overdrawn half the time. But I am rich in the word of God. I know what is in the bible and I know how to access the things I need. I am rich in mercy; I am rich in knowledge and in understanding the love of God. I believe that "Money Cometh" (title of a song from friends).

I have a testimony that happened just recently, since I have been editing this book. We needed a house payment. It was 4 days late. I have learned not to worry. I knew God knew about it, so I did not even pray about it. I didn't tell anyone. We went about our responsibilities, teaching at church, traveling, and being who we are.

On a Thursday night we were preparing for the service, which is a different way to do church, as we sit around a large table and share, teach, and pray. A new person had come that evening. Clifton had actually met him that day in a restaurant. After church he stayed until everyone was gone, and as Clifton was leaving, the new guy flagged Clifton down and handed him a canvas bag which was very heavy. Clifton said, "What is in here?" The man said "MONEY!"

There was more than enough money in there to make our house payment! How long has it been since someone chased you down to give you a bag of money? I can't get over it. And yet, that is just how our Father does things! I encourage you to give to God! Don't be a skeptic and think, "All they want over there at that church is my money." Renew your mind and give to God. Sow a seed. Prove God! In the area of money is the only place God says to "*try Him and see*" (see Malachi 3:10).

When the 700 Club came to our home and church, they came because someone had called them about Clifton's deliverance from alcohol testimony. After they came and talked to us, the interview and story turned into a financial testimony of the miracles God had done for us. We were living in a huge new home on 14 acres with no income. How did we live? God spoke to the saints! Many times, someone would come back our long drive way and have an envelope full of hundred-dollar bills, just when we needed house payment money, or even food.

One More Testimony

I have so many testimonies, but while editing I remembered this which is awesome! Scriptures I was given were these, when the miracle came:

Isaiah 61:7, Exodus 22:7, Zechariah 9:12, and I Timothy 5:17

DOUBLE!

While we were living in Indiana, we had paid a lot of money to the IRS and other places which we really did not even owe. It was a black mark on us, though, so we paid it, a little at a time. $11,000. Paid off, forgotten about.

Then we moved to Missouri. Our pay for our pastorate was not enough to live on. (Why did you accept the position? you ask.) We believed God had spoken to us to bring Grace to Southeast Missouri, and He never mentioned being paid to do it. So, as we struggled financially, we didn't say anything to anybody but God. We had been down this road before!

We received a phone call one day from a paralegal in Indiana. Clifton had been forced to apply for medical help when his "Trigeminal Neuralgia" and the medication he was taking caused him to be a zombie, unable to function. He applied for disability, as a temporary help until we could walk out of that darkness. He was turned down, so we just kept believing God and going forward as much as we knew how. This woman asked us how we were doing, and I told her we were awesome, Clifton had been healed through a medical procedure, and he had his life back! I told her we were pastoring full time and were so thankful.

She said we should apply for a "closed period" of benefits, because as she looked at our records, in her opinion, he was due the help. Clifton didn't have to do anything. She was going to go before a judge for him. We talked about it, and told her to "go for it". In a few weeks we received a check for over $22,000! She told us the judge said Clifton should never have been turned down in the first place. That money was double what was stolen from us! It carried us through.

Nugget #11

SPIRIT (HEART) TO MIND, NOT HEAD TO HEART

In the early days when I was first learning the word of God, I would hear preachers say something, then I began to teach it. Because I had heard it, I taught: "Now, we have to get what we have heard from the word of God from our heads down into our hearts. You receive in your head, but it has to get down into your heart." **NO**! That is the *opposite* of what happens!

One day my husband received the revelation that we already have ALL the word of God, the counsel of God in our hearts, in our spirits. When Jesus is invited into our hearts, He brings all the Word and Counsel of God. That is why – when you hear something you have never heard before – your SPIRIT is what grabs the truth, and you know that you know that you know! When Jesus comes in, He comes in with the entire counsel of God, and all of it resides on the inside of you. Your mind is what has to catch up! The first time he said that, I knew it was "truth." Also, if something is said that makes your spirit grieve, or you sense, as they say, a "check" in your spirit, then it's time to check it out for yourself in the word. When the truth is heard, your spirit "grabs" it with great force! "Truth" has been there all along.

The Apostle Paul was clear about renewing the mind. Let's look at Romans 12:2 (Amplified Bible): *"Do not be conformed to this world, this age, fashioned after and adapted to it's external, superficial customs. But be transformed (changed) by the entire renewal of your mind - by its new ideals and it's new attitude...."*

Then in Ephesians 4:23: *"And be constantly renewed in the spirit of your mind – having a fresh mental and spiritual attitude...."*

It Takes Faith!

Only the word of the Living God can give you this renewal! The world will not, CANNOT give you anything. One of the first times I heard God's voice was when I was reading Ephesians, about to burst with excitement, and I heard so clearly from the Holy Spirit, "If you've got the faith. I've got the power!"

From the book of Ephesians, we learn we are holy, blessed with every spiritual blessing, blameless, beloved, accepted, we have redemption, salvation, deliverance, grace, we have been chosen, and we have obtained an inheritance! And that is only the first chapter! It takes FAITH to believe this! Our minds must be renewed to receive this. Your heart knows it. Clifton says there is a filter in your mind, and it is clogged up! The spirit has a fountain of force, like a water hose, and it needs to blow out the filter in the clogged-up heads! He has always said he wanted to build a church that had a coat rack, a hat rack, and a **head** rack, where we could all leave our heads and receive the powerful word of God right straight into our hearts!

Renewing the mind is a "labor" we do to enter into rest. Hebrews 4:11, *"Let us therefore be diligent to enter that rest...."* When we work, God rests, but when we rest, God works! I did hear someone say that, and it stuck tight! Being such a "worker", I still struggle with "resting".

Our spirit is as perfect as it is ever going to be. Our heart (spirit) contains everything we need, we are complete, we are whole and healed. It is what we don't know that hurts us. We get born again, and then it is a life-long learning process to find out what we have. It is a treasure hunt to discover all God has given us. Our heart knows it. Our spirit has it. The mind is the last to come along.

This is a short nugget, but a powerful one, and one that will be a life changer if it is applied. I have been consistently teaching and preaching this "hidden treasure" for a number of years. It is probably one of the most impacting shifts you will make in your life.

Once you know how to "renew your mind", you will escape the tragedy of being a prisoner of what you "think" to be true, and be set free to be who you truly are in the realm of God's Kingdom! That is a "Wow"!

Nugget #12

THE VIRTUOUS WOMAN: THE CHURCH

The number 12 is God's number for government and authority. I mention this because it is something my heart is in tune to: God's numbers and their meanings. The Church should be the Authority! More recently I have been seeking and receiving revelation on the CHURCH of today. You and I as the CHURCH are supposed to be shining brightly! After all, we have Heaven within us and our calling is to let our light shine. Jesus said the "*Kingdom of Heaven is within us.*" I believe that since we have Heaven within us, we are to tell the world there is a better way to live than how we live. Jesus is real, He is always there for us. By faith we appropriate all the Kingdom of Heaven has to offer. So, as the church, we are to respond to Jesus as our Husband. Our Husband cares for us, protects us, was willing to give His life for us.

A few years ago, the Lord showed me something I had not heard from anyone! I taught it in Charis Bible College, after clearing my revelation with Andrew Wommack, founder and president of the bible college.

I was reading Proverbs 31, verses 10-31, and thinking of how difficult this is for a wife and mother to carry out! This woman is Super Woman! Then the Lord spoke to me. He said, "She is the Church. The Virtuous Woman is the Church." I saw how the wife's response to her "husband" is actually the church's response to Jesus, her Husband! And by the way, I have mentioned this before, but remember, we are ALREADY married to Jesus! Otherwise we could not legally be intimate with Him. And we are called to produce "fruit" from this intimate relationship the Lord desires from us. I have a friend who says, concerning this relationship we have with the Lord compared to the human relationship between a man and woman: "No covenant, no lovin' it, no wed, no bed." It makes sense that we are already married, the moment we believe.

This wonderful wisdom filled Book of Proverbs was written by the wisest man who ever lived! Solomon was writing about his mother. In the beginning of the book he is called "King Lemuel", and I have heard it taught that this was a "pet name" Bathsheba had for Solomon. I don't have a better explanation, so I am going with that. The first verse says this is a prophesy she taught him. I remember teaching my three sons these truths. "*Don't give your strength* (sex) *to women*." (verse 3) The first 9 verses are instruction to a leader. Then in verse 10, she shifts gears. This revelation came to me as I was teaching in the Bible College course on Proverbs. (Bob Yandian's book, <u>ONE</u>

<u>FLESH</u> was a resource I used then.)

I learned that verses 10-31 in Proverbs 31 is an acrostic. There are 22 letters in the Hebrew alphabet. Each verse has a Hebrew letter at the beginning of it, and a corresponding picture that goes with the verse.

THE VIRTUOUS WOMAN
PROVERBS 10-31
(KJV and NKJV)

Verse 10: "Who can find a virtuous woman?
For her price is far above rubies."

(This letter is Aleph, a picture of an ox. It speaks of prosperity, power, a leader. Whoever finds a virtuous woman is rich and powerful.)

"Virtuous" from the Webster's Dictionary: "Moral excellence in goodness, prudence, fortitude, temperance, and justice. Christian virtues are faith, hope, and love. Active power to accomplish a given effect. Chaste, pure."

The word "woman" is translated "wife" in the New KJV. A virtuous "church" is valuable! Her worth cannot be calculated, as it is "far above" rubies. Jesus loves the Church, and has given His life for it! Acts 20:28 says He purchased the Church with His own blood. This speaks of her value and worth. The virtuous (excellent) wife of a husband is worth more than jewels! Bathsheba is teaching Solomon the kind of woman he should have as a wife. In the same way, we as the body of Christ, the Church, ought to act like the valuable people we are!

Verse 11: "The heart of her husband safely trusts her;
So he will have no lack of gain." (NKJV)

(This letter is Beth, or Bet, and the picture is a home with one door, a family. Her husband can count on her, and does not need any outside relationship.)

Jesus trusts the Church. Stop and think about it, she is all He has on the earth to promote Him! He has no need for anything else. He has given His Bride everything. We, as the Church, possess all power and authority, just like Jesus. He has given it to us. He has no lack, and we have no lack. When I studied this portion of scripture as the Virtuous Woman being the wife, it is still true, that she is to be trusted, and her husband has no need to go outside the marriage because she will be all he needs. I propagate the marriage as the most wonderful relationship we can possess except for our relationship with our Creator.

Verse 12: "She does him good and not evil
All the days of her life."

(There are varied descriptions of this letter. It depends on the time frame, the culture, the age. I am using

Gimmel, a picture of a camel. A camel runs straight, not moving its head. Dependable. A camel does not look to the left or the right, but has its eyes on the goal ahead. It means to gather, to walk, to carry. It also means pride.)

This hardly needs explanation! As the Church, we are to represent Jesus in a truthful, positive way. Do the Church good! I know there are those reading this who don't go to church, or say they "are" the church. There are some who were hurt in church, or knew someone who had a bad experience, and on and on. HOWEVER!!! As a Pastor it is most hurtful and disappointing and a grief to the very core of our hearts that the "church" has been thrown out as unnecessary by so many. To "do the Church good" is to support it, go, and be involved in the passion of Jesus, which is to increase His Family! House churches sprung up after Jesus's resurrection, and they are springing up now, since the Charismatic movement started in the 1960's and 1970's. Now Grace has caused an increase in the number of house churches because sadly, many pastors do not preach the unconditional love of God for fear they will lose "control" of their people. Human beings now living and breathing need to know LOVE. They must have a confidence that God loves them, and they have worth and value to others. If love is not in place, the outcome of their lives is fear, guilt, shame, insecurity, and anything that brings condemnation to their minds and hearts.

We as individuals are the Church, as well as a group. When we were traveling full-time, we could not serve in a local church like we wanted to. But we always promoted the Church. Encouraging the saints to become members and serve with others. I advocate "trying" different churches till you find where you "fit." There is a place for you!

Verse 13: "She seeks wool and flax,
And willingly works with her hands."

(Daleth, or Dal is a picture of a tent door, and means to hang or to enter. Having what is needed.)

The Church always has what is needed in the season it is needed. Wool for the winter, flax for the summer clothing speaks of the "goods" always being there when needed. The Church uses our hands to reach out to those who need this clothing. It speaks here of providing what is needed at the TIME. We are also – as wives and mothers – to have what is needed for our families. With God's help we can provide, always the need at the time.

Verse 14: "She is like the merchant ships,
she brings her food from afar."

(This is the 5th letter, He – "hey" – and is a picture of a man with his hands raised. It means breath, look, reveal)

The Church as a "merchant ship" has the best there is to offer to their people. As a representative of Jesus, we as the Church need to search out the truth, bring it from different places, not just shop at one store. The truth is like a diamond or gold to be dug out, to be searched for, to be shopped for. The Church has the "food" each of us need. Not everyone needs the same thing the same day. But the Church has it all. As we go and listen, God has everything we need to hear that day coming from the people and the Pastor. We need to know what we *already have.* This scripture – in referring to the wife – says the same thing, that she shops for the best for her family.

Verse 15: "She also rises while it is yet night,
And provides food for her household,
And a portion for her maidservants."

(This letter is Waw and the picture is a tent peg. A secure hook. Again, something that can be counted on.)

In the days when I was teaching this to women as the way a wife was to be towards her husband, I thought, "No wonder she is Super Woman, she has maids!" So, I immediately hired myself a housekeeper! Then as revelation unfolded, I saw that as a wife and as a Church, we are to RISE UP in darkness and still provide for our household. In the bleakest of times, in the difficult circumstances, we still must provide the goods people need. It is not about us anyway, but it's

ALL about Jesus, the Church, and His Divine Plan. The Church can have joy in the midst of sorrow, and we can continue in faith when we don't see how this is ever going to work. There are those who look to us, the Church, for answers. We HAVE the answers, sometimes we may have to seek within ourselves and pray and trust God to reveal them to us. Save a portion for those who are not of the household. The maidservants are those who are serving, but maybe not realizing who they are in Christ, or not in the Body yet. We are to have a word in season for anyone crossing our paths.

Verse 16: "She considers a field and buys it;
From her profits she plants a vineyard."

(This letter is Zaiyn, and is a picture of a plough or a sword. It means food, cut, weapon, nourish.)

The Church, (YOU), considers (ponders upon, meditates upon) the field of people's hearts. The Church (Jesus is the Head) has paid the ultimate price to buy everyone's heart. We consider the field of a man's heart. We pay the price of self-sacrifice to win that person's heart to Jesus. We then plant into a vineyard. We plant into another field. We sow seed. The Church profits by people coming in to the fold in the realm of the Spirit. Every single person is of value, everybody is a gem to the Lord. This is the 7th verse in this acrostic, the 7th letter. Seven is perfection, completeness.

Verse 17: "She girds herself with strength,
And strengthens her arms."

(The letter is Has, and the picture is a tent wall. It means outside, divide, half. Also, this is a strong wall, a fortress.)

She prepares herself; she invests in herself; she clothes herself with power and authority. Both the wife and the Church. She strengthens her arms. She knows she needs strength to wrap her arms around her husband and others. The Church wraps her arms around the whole world.

Verse 18: "She perceives that her merchandise is
good,
And her lamp does not go out by night."

(The letter is Thath, and the picture is a basket. It means surround and contain.)

The Church knows she has the goods. Just like a confident woman knows she has all it takes to minister to her family. The lamp of the Church burns through the night of sorrow, pain, grief, suffering, dark times. It never goes out because the lamp is Jesus. He is the Light. A wife and mother's light burns through the dark times, always there for her family. A godly woman always has the goods, because she knows God, knows His word, and trusts in Him.

Verse 19: "She stretches out her hands to the distaff',
And her hand holds the spindle."

(The letter is Yod, and the picture is a hand and an arm. It means work, throw, and worship.)

The Church, (and the virtuous woman) ministers to the family. The distaff is the staff for holding the flax or wool for spinning. This speaks of a woman's work, authority, or domain. Her hand also holds this spindle, which speaks of her authority. The Church has Authority. Jesus has seen to it, and the Church will rise in the last days and take her rightful place. We reign in righteousness with Him.

Verse 20: "She extends her hand to the poor,
Yes, she reaches out her hands to the needy."

(The letter is Kaph, and the picture is the open palm of the hand. It means bend, open, allow, and home.)

This is an open hand, reaching out to the world, laying hands on them for healing and deliverance. This is our calling as a Church, and as a virtuous woman representing Jesus. Reaching out is the purpose of the Church today. As a wife and mother, we are to always have an open hand, giving to those in our homes. Extending ourselves unselfishly to provide what is needed concerning our husbands and children.

The Virtuous Woman: The Church

Verse 21: "She is not afraid of snow for her household,
For all her household is clothed in scarlet."

(The letter is Lam. Picture is a shepherd's staff, meaning teach, yoke, toward.)

The scarlet here is representative of the blood of Jesus. A Virtuous woman and the Church make sure everyone in the house knows about the blood of Jesus and it's saving and delivering power. The Church has no fear of cold, dead religion when the blood is preached. May I add that we as wives and mothers should have no fear when it comes to our household becoming saved, born again. We have the promise from Acts 16:31, *"Believe on the Lord Jesus Christ, and you will be saved, you and your household."* Of course, they will be making their own decision, but God will – has already – moved Heaven and Earth to save your family! He knows how to arrange circumstances to bring them to Himself. Even in their last moments of life, before their last breath, He can and will show up for them and give them the opportunity to say "Yes" to Jesus. Who can resist His unconditional love?

Verse 22: "She makes herself coverings of tapestry;
Her clothing is silk and purple." (KJV)

(The letter is Mem, a picture of water. It means mighty and blood. It eludes to relationships, because

144

of the points on the letter.)

The Church has woven for itself beautiful coverings of tapestry. Tapestry is a hand-woven heavy rug or wall hanging, or a furniture covering. Symbolically the Church has handwoven beautiful scripture, poems, and songs, and made it a place of peace and comfort. A woman makes for herself a life of strength, honor, and wisdom for everyone to see. She does this by trusting the Lord, and by exemplifying faith.

Verse 23: "Her husband is known in the gates,
When he sits among the elders of the land."

(This letter is Nan, and the picture is a sprouting seed. It means to continue, heir, and son.)

The Virtuous woman's husband is known because of her. Jesus is known by the actions and beliefs of the Church. The gates of the city are where government was conducted. We looked at this a little in the story of Ruth. The elders gathered there to do business, to decide matters pertaining to the people of the city. When a woman had virtue and notoriety among the people, it was a feather in the cap of her husband. Jesus is known in the gates as we are ambassadors for Him. As the Church shines, Jesus shines. As the Church is reaching out to all, and loving, and showing grace, it makes Jesus desirable. As wives, sometimes we can "make or break" our husbands. There have been countless men of God we have met over our many years of ministry who were anointed and had great knowledge. Some of them we were not comfortable to have in our church to speak because of their wives. Sad but true. A godly wife covers for her husband, respects his call, and treats him well in public, as well as at home.

Verse 24: "She makes linen garments and sells them,
And supplies sashes for the merchants."

(The letter is Xan, and the picture is a thorn. It means to grab and protect.)

The Church, as well as the virtuous woman, or wife, is busy doing her part to keep things going. In our time now, the Church has received the revelation of Grace where we know we are righteous, and we don't "work" to obtain anything from God. However, after we know who we are, and what we have because of what Jesus accomplished for us on the cross, we are to "REST" in Him, and do things because of what we have, not to strive to receive something. This speaks of the Church providing linen garments, a picture of pureness, of holiness. A lot of folks throw out holiness now that they have grace, but holiness is vital for our lives. What is holiness? "Condition or character of being holy. (spiritually perfect, saintly, and godly") And the Bible declares we are holy when we believe what Jesus did for us. We are saints. We are righteous. This is all expounded upon in the first chapter of Ephesians. The verse here speaks of the Church supplying needs in the marketplace.

Verse 25: "Strength and honor are her clothing;
She shall rejoice in time to come."

(The letter is On, and the picture is an eye. It means to watch and to know.)

The Church is clothed in strength and honor. Jesus has seen to it. I realize that some churches don't know who they are, and don't operate this way, but it is true, nevertheless. She, the Church, will rejoice, and rejoices now, as these verses are prophetic. The greatest rejoicing is yet to come, but we can start now. We can have great joy, and an abundance of good times sharing our faith, and seeing the glory of the Church shine forth from it as the bright light God made it! We, the Church, are the Hope of the world! As a wife, my strength is Jesus. I do rejoice in the future. The saying "The best is yet to come" is a true statement! I encourage women to have vision, to have a dream of how they want their family to be, and praise the Lord daily that this is God's will, and that the vision will come to pass!

Verse 26: "She opens her mouth with wisdom,
And on her tongue is the law of kindness."

(The letter is Pah or Pey and the picture is an open mouth.)

The Virtuous Woman – the Church – is kind, wise, and speaks with grace and love. Also, the woman who is being a virtuous wife treats her husband this way. Remember that "*love never fails.*" Speaking with kindness defuses a potentially explosive situation. The book of James says that the tongue is a fire, and that it is set on fire by hell, and that it is evil, unruly and full of poison. (see James 3:6 & 8) A tongue under the influence of the Holy Spirit is kind and loving, and speaks with wisdom. This is a hard lesson for some of us. It was for me. I heard from the spirit of God to be very slow to speak in some situations. It takes God to slow us down, but it will work to the good of the one following the instruction of the Lord.

Verse 27: "She watches over the ways of her household,
And does not eat the bread of idleness."

(The letter is Tsad, the picture of a path, a destination. The meaning is trail, journey, and hunt.)

The Church watches over her household of faith. She does not get stagnant or stuck. I believe if we as the body of Christ, the Church, would not be "idle" but obey the Great Commission: "*Go into all the world and preach the gospel to every creature*", there would be no time to be idle and get into false teaching or lethargy. (Neither would the church people have time to be offended, or find fault every time they turn around.) The picture here of a "path" speaks of our life, moving in a direction. We are on a journey. Our destination is Heaven, but we have a life of "destiny" to fulfill here on earth. Why were we born? For a purpose, for a reason, to be a light to the world! Everyone can find their place. If you need help, don't hesitate to talk to someone you trust. God is more than willing to reveal His plan for your life! And it's never too late!

Verse 28: "Her children rise up and call her blessed; Her husband also, and he praises her."

(The letter is Qap, and is a picture of the sun at horizon. It means condense, circle, and time. Another picture I found was the back of the head, which I like, because this praise we are reading about from the verse is the children and husband praising her behind her back, not to her face.)

When I was still teaching this as a literal mother and wife, I would tell this story: my kids, after they grew up, and that "rise up" is GROW UP – they would tell other people what a blessing it was for them to have me as a mom. They did not say that to me when they were growing up under my leadership! They praised me after they left our home. And my husband began to praise me, too. Now look at it from the standpoint of the Virtuous Woman being the Church, and her response to Jesus has been so awesome that her husband Jesus praises her! The children also are seeing the Church as a blessing.

Verse 29: "Many daughters have done well,
But you excel them all."

(The letter is Resh, and the picture is a man's head, his face. He is telling her to her face how excellent she is. It means first, top, beginning.)

In the natural we all want to hear this praise from our husbands. "You are the most excellent." I shared in the marriage teaching how my own husband told me he did NOT love me, but in the end he was telling me how he loved me more than ever, that I was the best wife in the world, and that he thought I was truly a "virtuous woman." Jesus says this about His Bride. He loves the Church with an everlasting love. It was a "great mystery," the Apostle Paul called it in Ephesians 5, that Jesus and the Church were one, as the husband and wife are to be "one flesh."

Verse 30: "Charm is deceitful and beauty is passing,
But a woman who fears the Lord, she shall be
praised."

(The letter is Shan, and the picture is teeth. Sharp, press, eat, two.)

Anyone can be charming and pleasant for a short period of time, but it takes the strength of God to live out the character God has designed for us to live in and by. This scripture is telling us that any woman who shows reverence for God and keeps His ways will be praised by those around her. The Church is designed to show forth the glory and honor of God Himself. I think also the "sharp" meaning eludes to a sharpness in her words to bring a dividing of truth. *"Rightly dividing the word of truth"* (II Tim 2:15). "Two" in the meaning of the letter speaks of the woman and her God. In the natural, also, the husband and his wife are two becoming one.

Verse 31: "Give her of the fruit of her hands,
And let her own works praise her in the gates."

(The letter is Tau and the picture is two crossed sticks, signifying the signing of something. A signature. The final word.)

Everyone who works with their hands receives rewards. There is fruit from labor. Let the Church's works praise her. The Church will be praised in the gates, at the entry way into Heaven, and also on earth. We as women, or we as the Church, do not have to promote ourselves, because our works shine forth, and everyone sees.

The Hebrew letter for this verse is "the signature", or Tau. The last thing we do is our signature when we have made a deal. The Church will not have to do a thing to be noticed or seen. Her glory will be seen by all. Her works will praise her. Her fruit will be obvious to the universe! This day is near, and is already shining forth in many places in the world. The virtuous wife and mother also will be praised because of her works, without any bragging on herself!

In Conclusion...

This chapter is truly a "nugget" compared to all the revelation that is available on the subject of the Virtuous Woman, as the Church, the wife, mother, and business woman. My prayer is that you have gleaned something to help you in your own daily life and/or ministry.

Nugget # 13
PSALM 42: "HOPE IN GOD"

This will help you when in distress. A few days after my mother went to Heaven, I was sitting in her chair thinking and praying, and God dropped this Psalm into my heart. He gave me a message to deliver to a Methodist Church group in Illinois where I had been invited to speak.

Verses 1 and 2

"As the deer pants for the water brooks,
So pants my soul for you O God.

My soul thirsts for God, for the living God.
When shall I come and appear before God?"

Does your soul pant for the presence of God like a deer wants to drink water? From the time I was born again, I have thirsted for the things of God. Before we receive, we are hungry, thirsty to see God and His power, His love. David is wanting to know when he will again get to go to the temple and worship. Those of us who love to worship and love the church know what this means to have a longing to go to the place where we feel God the strongest. In those days, there was not an indwelling of the Spirit. They had to seek Him out. Today we can find God where ever we look! We don't have to wait till church time! God does fill the hungry soul, though. He sees your heart when it is panting after Him, and He comes to you! In these days, he lives in us, and we have all he has provided at our disposal, at our fingertips at all times.

Verses 3 and 4

"My tears have been my food day and night,
While they continually say to me,
Where is your God?"

When I remember these things,
I pour out my soul within me.
For I used to go with the multitude;
I went with them to the house of God,
With the voice of joy and praise,
With a multitude who kept a pilgrim feast."

Anyone who has been in a situation where grief has overcome you, you understand what the Psalmist is saying. I cry till I have no more tears. And friends and relatives are saying, "I thought you were a believer. I thought your prayers would be answered." That is how they say, "Where is your God?" Where is this God you have been talking about? I thought you said He would come through for you." He is saying he used to go into the congregation with them, and he used to be praising the Lord. He kept the feasts. He was happy then. All of us know a time when we were so excited about knowing the Lord Jesus. People and circumstances can bring us down. In these "now" times, we have the indwelling of the Holy Spirit, and we are never alone. He is as close as our very breath, and He has already placed us in the heavenly realm.

Verse 5

"Why are you so cast down, O my soul?
And why are you disquieted within me?
Hope in God, for I shall yet praise Him
For the help of His countenance."

Why have you been thrown down, O my soul? He speaks to himself. Why are you upset, why do you allow these outside situations to cause you to be depressed? Then he answers himself: HOPE IN GOD! He will speak of the mercies of the Lord, and he will praise the Lord anyway, for the "help of His countenance." The very countenance of God is this: "Expression of the face, indicating mental calmness and composure. Expression of approval, favor and aid." (Webster's Dictionary) So, he knows he will receive aid, favor and help from the One he praises when there is opportunity for discouragement.

Verse 6

"O my God, my soul is cast down within me;

Therefore I will remember You from the land of the
Jordan,
And from the heights of Hermon,
From the Hill Mizar."

Because my soul has been cast down, or thrown aside due to heavy burdens, I must remember some great things from before. I will remember the land of Jordan, a fruitful pleasant place, and I climbed Mt Hermon, he says, which is the highest mountain in Syria. I saw this mountain while in Israel! It is so high; they have a ski slope and snow! He could see then, afar off, and know when the enemy was coming. He could also see the handiwork of God, his Deliverer. Let's look now at the enemy and get rid of him! We, like this writer, need to remember some good things when our circumstances are making us sad. *"Therefore I remind you to stir up the gift of God."* (II Peter 1:6) Every one of us have some great victories and good memories we can bring to the forefront of our thinking, and pull ourselves up by our bootstraps with the help of the Holy Ghost!

Verse 7

"Deep calls unto deep at the noise of Your waterfalls;
All Your waves and billows have gone over me."

Deep thoughts, deep remembrances call to the deep as concerning the Spirit of God. The noise of the waterfalls are wonderful sounds, and God is speaking now. The writer knows how to write about the deepest condition of the human heart. He gets some reprieve. The waves of compassion and billows of love and peace flow over him. These waves flow over us as we come into the presence of God and resist the lies and oppression brought to our minds by the enemy of our soul.

Verse 8

*"The Lord will command His
lovingkindness in the daytime,
And in the night His song shall be with me -
A prayer to the God of my life."*

The Lord HAS commanded His lovingkindness towards all His children. The writer is feeling this now, and we can also feel it. We can know beyond a doubt that God's lovingkindness is hovering over us, enveloping us. It is coming from the inside of us. In the night time, in the dark, He gives us a song. God always gives a song. Music is a demon buster! Then we have the last line, "a prayer to the God of my life." This is verse #8, the number for New Beginnings. A new beginning is starting here, because the psalmist is recognizing the presence of God, and now things will change!

Verse 9

"I will say to God my Rock,

'Why have You forgotten me?
Why do I go mourning because
of the oppression of the enemy?'"

Evidently his victory is short lived. Does this sound like anyone you know? It sounds like a lot of people I know! We get through one valley, and the same enemy brings the same oppression as before. We forget our joy from the last time God delivered us and showed up. But he sees something here. He does accuse God of forgetting him, but he also is asking himself, *"Why do I go mourning because of the oppression of the enemy?"* This is something we can ask ourselves. Why do we do this when we have been given billows of love and waterfalls of kindness? He is present, and has given us a song and a prayer.

Verse 10

"As with a breaking of my bones
My enemies reproach me.
While they say to me all day long
'Where is your God?'"

The number 10 is the number for trials. This guy is in pain! The reproach of his enemies is like bones breaking! It brings great suffering for his enemies to say, "Where is your God?" We all suffer these persecutions. Knowing Him, though, as we do today, by the love and power of the Holy Ghost makes it bearable. And also, not just bearable, but we come

Nuggets from the Gold Mine

out on the other side with complete victory! Everyone reading this has "war stories" of unrighteous persecution. But the psalmist goes back in the next verse to his original statement, and ends his song of yearning for God while in a state of deep grief.

Verse 11

"Why are you so downcast O my soul?
And why are you disquieted within me?
Hope in God
For I shall yet praise Him.
The help of my countenance and my God."

The number 11 equals restoration, 10 plus 1. This is a verse of restoration. Look at the last verse. He has come to the conclusion that his own countenance will help him now. The expression was his own, "Expression of the face, indicating mental calmness and composure. Expression of approval, favor, and aid." He has received the hope for his soul. It is a thread that runs throughout the word of God to praise Him anyway, even in the midst of tribulation. HOPE. "Confident expectation of good."

Nugget 14

PSALM 84: "PASSING THROUGH"

A very long time ago I was in a pitiful situation. I dwelt in the Psalms to receive comfort and peace. I had heard messages on Psalm 84 about the "valley of weeping." Since I was weeping and wailing during this particular season of my life, I latched onto that idea. I was in the valley of weeping – deep sigh! But one night in the middle of the night I happened to catch just a glimpse of a preacher whom I would never have listened to, but before I could shut him off, I heard him say, "It's not the valley of weeping we should look at here, but rather the two previous words, "passing through." I was impacted! A light went off! Yes! Let us **pass through** this valley of weeping!

My Heart and My Flesh Cry Out

Let's look at this Psalm. I taught on Psalms in my classes in Charis Bible College in Colorado. The Lord gave me so many great comparisons to parallel these Old Testament truths to the New testament revelation we now have. The Psalmist David begins here with:

Verses 1-2

"How lovely is your tabernacle,
O Lord of hosts!
My soul longs, yes, even faints
for the courts of the Lord;
My heart and my flesh cry out
for the living God."

This is a prerequisite for receiving from God. I am not talking about works, and I am not even talking about stuff you "must do" to receive. However, I do know that God likes it a lot when we love His place of worship (church) and when our very soul longs for and cries out for Him. Anywhere the Lord is, is "lovely." I do go and worship Him in my woods, on the ocean, in the mountains, anywhere I can, and some of you may think that IS where we should worship. As a side note, I am grieved that there are thousands of believers quitting church, stopping their support to the organized church, and feeling like they have no responsibility to be together with other believers. As I have followed those "unbelieving believers", it turns out they should have stayed with the congregation and received counsel, accountability, and fellowship. I am sad that lives fall apart when they don't have to, when there is help available. Pride is a killer. Consider what I say, I believe it is straight from the Holy Spirit!

Verses 3-4:

"Even the sparrow has found a home,
and the swallow a nest for herself,
Where she may lay her young –
Even your alters, O Lord of hosts,
My King and my God.
Blessed are those who dwell in your house;
They will still be praising You. Selah."

The first thing I thought when I read this was, "Even a birdbrain knows enough to make a nest and bring her children to the house of God!" Yes, even the sparrow has access. She is free and also secure as she builds her nest, her "safe place" for her babies. We need the church. We need the "tabernacle of the Lord of Hosts." Jesus went to synagogue, He showed up every week! He was teaching how important it is by His actions.

David writes here of those who dwell in "Your house" being blessed, meaning they have favor, it is a blessed thing to be in the presence of God! "They will still be praising You", I believe, speaks of no matter what else happens, those who know Him intimately will still praise in the midst of adversity.

These pilgrims are coming to the feast of Tabernacles in Jerusalem. They are thirsting for the house of God.

Verses 5-6

"Blessed is the man whose strength is in You,
Whose heart is set on pilgrimage,
As they pass through the Valley of Baca,
They make it a spring;
The rain also covers it with pools."

Anyone who has strength in God is blessed, favored, and prosperous! His heart is set on continuing and finishing the journey. Many obstacles are in our way, we who are walking through this world to get to eternity. We will "pass through" at least one wilderness, the "Valley of Weeping." Baca means "weeping." Baca is a plant, balsam, which survives in the desert.

We as people of the Most High must learn how to "pass through" these desert places, or experiences. They come, we encounter them, but the mistake we make is building our home there, planting a garden, and nailing pictures on the wall. No, move on through, keep praising, keep on worshiping. As the verse says, make it a spring! Make lemonade out of that lemon!

We all have dry places where we may not hear a thing from God. But this portion of scripture says that the rain covers it with "pools", or blessings. There are blessings in your wilderness, your desert. God loves us and desires to get us through this life as an ambassador for Him. He will give us blessings in the midst of the desert. I know how it sounds, but it is the truth!

Verses 7-8

"They go from strength to strength;
Each one appears before God in Zion.
Oh Lord God of hosts, hear my prayer;
Give ear, O God of Jacob! Selah"

We gain strength from our trials. He is telling us that those who make our wilderness a "spring" will be strong, and we will appear before God in Zion, the church! Keeping a good attitude during hardship is a sign you are hanging out at the pool...water...the word. Reading and meditating on God's word is one way to make your wilderness a pool of water. You will be refreshed instead of looking like you have been through a storm. As God's representatives we should keep in the forefront of our thinking that we need to still be a witness to the goodness of our God. People do see you. They do take notice. I ask myself often if I would want to have what I have if I was an onlooker, searching for truth. How do I rate as a "light to the world?" Am I salt, causing thirst for the lost? Or do they look at me and say, "Who needs this, I already have what she has." (Discouragement, lack, sadness.) The God we serve always has a pool, always has a refreshing, always is ready and willing to walk us through to the other side in victory!

Verses 9-10

"O God, behold our shield,
And look upon the face of Your anointed.
For a day in Your courts is better than a thousand.
I would rather be a doorkeeper in the house of my
God
Than dwell in the tents of wickedness."

How prophetic! "Your anointed" speaks of our Messiah! He was prophesied as our "Shield" way back all those years before He came to earth. A day in the courts of God is better than a thousand days anywhere else! He would rather stand in the doorway of God's house than have a dwelling with the wicked. Some of you may think you are just on the outskirts, at the door of God's plan, His anointing, but you still would rather be there than go back to the way you used to live, even if the outward appearance looks good. Nice big home, fancy car, and "stuff". You have learned it is not fulfilling. Only God's plan brings peace. He wants us all to come on in, not just stand in the doorway!

Verses 11-12

"For the Lord God is a sun and shield;
The Lord will give grace and glory;
No good thing will He withhold
From those who walk uprightly.
O Lord of hosts

Psalm 84: "Passing Through"

Blessed is the man who trusts in you!"

I teach Psalms through New Testament glasses. Yes, the Lord God is most assuredly a sun and shield! He *"has given"* (past tense) the grace and glory and we have it, we can walk in it every day when we know what we have. He withholds no good thing. We learn from the Apostle Paul that since God did not withhold Jesus, why would He not "freely give us all things?"

This has become a part of my daily life. I might be a fanatic, but I get results! I am so thrilled at what God has done for me. We can all be on "Cloud 9" with knowing Him and His great benefits. He said He would not withhold from those who "walk uprightly." This is where folks say "Oh, but I'm not upright."

The truth is, YES, you are if you are a believer in the Lord Jesus! You have been made righteous, remember the Grace nugget? Never allow the enemy of your soul to place condemnation on you and cause you to doubt your righteousness.

The man, woman and child who trusts in God is blessed, says the last line of the Psalm: "happiness or welfare, good fortune, divine favor, extremely pleasing, highly agreeable, being in heaven, enjoying bliss" (Webster's Dictionary)

This is a description of the one who trusts, or has faith in God! Faith is simply believing what God has said enough to act on it. "*Faith without works is dead*."

I was extremely blessed when I saw this revelation that we are to "pass through" this valley of weeping! I trust it will help you who read this.

Nugget #15
HEALING

There came a time when the Word of God was so illuminated to me that every time I received a revelation, the whole Bible seemed to be about that subject! One of the first of these truths that jumped off the page at me was concerning healing. I heard some teaching on the subject. It was alive and powerful to both my husband and me, and we began to lay hands on the sick, as the word said to do. We saw miracle after miracle, as well as recovery healings. (Mark 16:18: "...*they will lay hands on the sick, and they will recover.*")

My tooth was throbbing every time my heart beat, and it was sensitive to cold and heat, and I was in pain. I had been complaining around the time we first were convinced it was God's will to heal our physical bodies. We were in the car, and Clifton was driving. He reached across and laid his hand on my face and prayed. Miraculously the pain stopped and that tooth lasted for years. We were amazed. This was the beginning of our 43-year healing ministry!

I want to show you the scriptures we found in the

beginning. We had been in a church that did not believe it was "always" God's will to heal people. According to His word, it IS ALWAYS His will to heal. "Jesus healed them all."

Matthew 4:24

"Then His fame went throughout all Syria; and they brought to Him all sick people who were afflicted with various diseases and torments, and those who were demon possessed, epileptics, and paralytics; and He healed them all."

How exciting is this for a sick person?! Most Christians read this and think, "That was then." But Jesus did say that we would do the works that He did and "greater works" because He was going to His Father.

John 14:12

"Most assuredly I say to you, he who believes in Me, the works that I do, he will do also; and greater works than these will he do, because I go to My Father."

So, this is not just the disciples, but "he who believes in Me", He said. That's you and me!

Isaiah 53:5

"But He was wounded for our transgressions, He was bruised for our iniquities: the chastisement of our

peace was upon Him, and with His stripes we are healed." (KJV)

There was a lot of arguing going on between us and "religious people" when we first began to lay hands on the sick, and tell everyone we met that God still heals today! They said this meant "spiritual healing, not physical healing." However, no, it says, "by His stripes we are healed." He took 39 stripes on His back for the healing of all our diseases. And as we read in Matthew just now, this also covers any ailment a person can have.

I Peter 2:24 brings the scripture from Isaiah over into the New Testament.

"...who Himself bore our sins in His own body on the tree, that we, having died to sins, might live for righteousness - by whose stripes you were healed."

Do you see that it is past tense? "You **were** healed." So, you were healed on the cross when Jesus paid the price for it, just like He paid the price for our sin. It is a package deal, a "bundle."

Jesus said in Luke 4:18: (Quoting from Isaiah)

"The Spirit of the Lord is upon Me, Because he has anointed Me To preach the gospel to the poor; He has sent me to heal the brokenhearted, To proclaim liberty to the captives And recovery of sight to the blind, To

set at liberty those who are oppressed; To proclaim the acceptable year of the Lord."

Psalms 107:20

"He sent His word and healed them, and delivered them from their destructions."

This verse is located in Book Five of the Books of Psalms. Five is God's number for grace. Healing is a product of His grace towards us. No one "deserves" to be healed. Healing is the "children's bread." God has provided it for us through love.

Everyone can be healed. The question arises, "Why isn't everyone healed?" I am glad I am not too proud to say a simple, "I don't know." I know it is God's will, I know it is paid for, I know He desires to see His children walk in healing just like we want to see our own children healed, whole, and blessed. We will know all our answers when we get to Heaven.

I believe we should always pray for all who express a desire for healing of their bodies. "What if they are not healed?" (A question I am often asked when I am encouraging people to pray for the sick.) What if they ARE?! A life changer for them and their loved ones.

The only reason more bodies aren't healed is because we aren't praying for enough of them! The more people you pray for, the more healing you will see.

One of the first ladies I prayed for died. She was advanced in a cancer illness, in the hospital, and on her way out. I was new to the healing revelation, but I prayed fervently, and thought I felt the anointing to heal her. When she passed away instead of rising up healed, I thought, "I'm never praying for anybody again."

Wrong thought! We need to say, "God, I don't understand, but I still trust You, and I will pray for the next sick person I have the opportunity to pray for." Hence, many, many healings have taken place in our ministry.

More than one person has risen up from a wheelchair, we have seen terminal cancerous victims healed, and many epileptics have been seizure free since one prayer! Countless wonderful healings, supernaturally, with death sentences from the doctors. Then also many teeth filled, broken bones healed immediately, heel spurs dissolved within minutes, and on and on I could go.

I am convinced that all we need to do is have a little faith to believe that God's word is true and act on it. I stopped arguing with anyone about whether God heals today. Everybody has the right to believe whatever they choose. But I have the call to preach the truth to all who will have ears to hear. (Or eyes to read!) Healing of the physical body is available to us today. There are instantaneous healings, and there are recovery healings. And if Doctors are involved there is NO condemnation! Doctors are friends of believers!

I recommend you to look up the scriptures on Healing. Read the Bible for yourself. I pray this nugget will cause you to be interested, and that you will pursue the truth.

I have been healed over and over, and presently walk in divine health at the age of 72. I did inherit good health and positive vibes concerning life from my mother and my grandmother. But I have also had opportunity to be sick. I have had "pre-cancer" spoken over me. That was in 1979. I never went back to the Doctor to see about it. We prayed and I had the confidence that cancer could not live in me! I "felt" the power flow through my body, but we don't necessarily need to "feel" anything.

Then, more recently I had severe pain, numbness and tingling in my shoulder, arm, and hand. I screamed into a towel it was so painful, usually in the middle of the night. I ran hot water over my arm, I took pain meds, but nothing helped. I would stand and swing my arm to take my mind off the excruciating pain. I went for prayer in a healing meeting in St Louis. We had, of course, prayed as well here at home. I did not "feel" anything at the time, but I believed I was healed. I don't know when the healing took place, for sure, but soon I noticed my arm, shoulder and hand were pain free and I was not suffering anymore!

I had migraine headaches for years as stress would go unchecked. I would have to go to BED, NO noise, NO light, NO food, NO nothing! I sought God for healing. I took no meds. Anyway, about 15 years ago I had my last one. A situation at church had me nearly dead with stress and sadness. I was in bed vomiting, crying with this type of headache. I can't tell you a "formula", but I can tell you that I was delivered and that was that. I have not had a hint of a headache of any kind since then. (And, trust me, there has been plenty of stress since then!) But I do, and have always, since I read the scriptures I gave you, believe in the Healing power of God and that He wants His kids well, just as we desire that for our own children.

My husband, also, is a walking miracle from being healed from several death sentences. At 76, he still does everything we ever did as ministers: travel, pastor, teach and "out and about witnessing" every day.

As I finish the editing in this book, May 2020, I have a medical issue! I am standing in faith for my left knee to be healed! I will have a procedure done soon, hopefully the pain will be taken care of! Remember God always wants His children well and healthy! Doctors are a blessing from God!

Nugget # 16
ISAIAH 58

We are going to look at Isaiah 58 through New Testament glasses. There is a ton of revelation here, and a solid foundation for any individual, church, or ministry. We have made this chapter a foundation for our 50-year Soul Winning Ministry. (Before we even knew it was in the bible!)

Clifton and I discovered this teaching early, and have taught on it for 43 years, ever since we went into full-time ministry. It has recently been refreshed to me, and I see the "now" application for the final wave or revival, awakening, or whatever you want to call it. There is a fresh tsunami of Holy Ghost on the horizon! Those with eyes will see. I see! Some will think it only thundered, and not "hear" the voice of God. Pray for yourself that you hear the voice of God.

Verse one of Isaiah 58 from the KJV says this: "*Cry aloud, spare not, lift up thy voice like a trumpet, and shew my people their transgressions, and the house of Jacob their sins.*"

I am sure this was not a message Isaiah wanted to

deliver. Think about it! Like a trumpet he was to shout out the sins of the people, God's people! Then the narrative continues... saying that the people sought God daily, they wanted justice, they took delight in approaching God. The not-so-good thing was they were doing it all out of "self-righteousness". Then in verse 3 they begin to whine. *"Haven't you seen that we have fasted? Don't you know that we have afflicted our souls, and you don't even notice?"*

Then God said, *"Do you call this a fast? Do you think I would call a fast for you to afflict your souls, to bow down your head, to spread sackcloth and ashes? Do you call this an acceptable day of the Lord?"*

Beginning in verse 6 is when God lowers the boom on them! He begins to tell them of the *fast He has chosen*! And it is this: The new testament gospel. The way of the Lord Jesus: *"to loose the bands of wickedness, to undo the heavy burdens, and to let the oppressed go free, and break every yoke."*

Verse 7: *"...deal thy bread to the hungry, bring the poor that are cast out into thy house, when you see the naked, cover him, and hide not thyself from thine own flesh."* (Your family)

Now, you have to grasp this: Verse 8 (new beginnings) *"Then shall thy light break forth as the morning, and thine health shall spring forth speedily: and thy righteousness shall go before thee; the glory of the*

Lord shall be thy rear reward."

We have to talk about this for a minute. This is a "wow". This takes some meditation. This is powerful and also hard to reconcile with "grace" where we know that we do not "work" for our blessings. It looks like we "do" and then "receive" in this scripture.

I am interjecting something here: there is a way to "walk" - or live - that will bring good things into your life. Just "knowing grace" does not bring the abundant life. I am convinced that when we truly have the revelation of God's GRACE, and His love for us, we are acting out of the heart of God. Too many believers I know are struggling with the message, grabbing at the teaching, because it truly is the "too good to be true" gospel, but IT IS TRUE!

"Knowing" is an intimate term used in the Word of God. We need to "know" to the point that we MOVE on it, act like we believe!

Fasting

Before we continue in these verses, I want to say something about "fasting." It seems to be a dirty word among, especially, "grace people." May I say, it is a new testament term, a new testament practice. The first time I fasted, I had no idea what I was doing. A spirit-filled friend told me we needed to "fast" for Clifton to answer his call to ministry. He was, at that time, "backslidden" according to the denomination where we had served. He was drinking, smoking, not going to church. We had planned a get together at another friend's house on Friday night. She said, "Lets fast for him, liquids only until Friday." This was on a Wednesday. I complied, again, totally ignorant. We were invited on Friday to friends for supper and card playing. (Complete story in ROSE book)

I drank only water and other liquids from Wednesday to Friday, and decided I would eat the supper being prepared for us on Friday night. Of course, Clifton knew nothing about any of this, that we had planned to get him into a meeting with a Pentecostal preacher. (Laugh!)

That night he was filled with the Holy Ghost, on the floor for two hours and forty-five minutes, (having been "slain in the Spirit) saw visions, heard the voice of God, answered the 5-year call on his life to ministry, and came up from there delivered from alcohol, nicotine, healed from serious back problems, (was told he would be in a wheelchair by the time he was 40), and completely healed of ulcers. "Geri, are you trying to tell me that all that happened because you fasted?" I am not going to answer your question!

The second time I fasted, I drank only water for three days. I was believing for direction, as we had been pastoring for about three years, and we felt "stuck". At the end of that time, God illuminated the scripture to me in the book of John where Jesus said He "*must go to other cities also*" …. That was a major message from the Holy Spirit. We soon were invited to places all over the area. Then to places across the United States and even overseas.

There are many different ways to fast. The idea is to deny yourself a pleasure. Deny yourself food, or a favorite delicacy. Many churches call a "Daniel's Fast" for 21 days at the beginning of the new year, which essentially proclaims "no pleasant bread." This takes your mind off food, and makes you remember Jesus! The "no pleasant bread" consists of vegetables mostly, as the three Hebrew children were instructed to eat while they turned down the King's rich foods.

Fasting is not a "work" we do to receive from God. I am just giving my testimony. Remember that God speaks to every one of His children. We must all "work out our own salvation" as we read in the new testament. Every person is different, every person hears from God in a personal way. The key is to "listen" and to follow the Spirit's leading. He is always on your side. One of Clifton's signature sayings is, "Remember, God is always for you, and never against you."

Final Points

Continuing now with verses 9-10: Isaiah prophesies that God will answer you when you call, saying "*Here*

I am." He continues with when we "*draw out our soul to the hungry, and satisfy the afflicted soul, then our light will rise in obscurity and our darkness shall be as the noonday.*"

Verse 11: "*And the Lord shall guide you continually, and satisfy your soul in drought, and make fat your bones: and you shall be like a watered garden, and like a spring of water whose waters fail not.*"

This is a foreshadowing of our walk with Jesus. All these things are true! You have an everlasting water supply. We are washed by the water of the word, Ephesians says. That water "never fails"!

~~~ THE END ~~~

A Note from Geri

Thank you for reading my <u>Nuggets from the Gold Mine</u> book. It has taken me a very long time to put it together. I've added, rewritten, and updated through the years, most recently in 2020, so I believe it is up to date. I did not expound on the most recent "virus scare". That will be saved for my final book, a daily devotional I have worked on for the past 20 years.

My previous book, <u>Your Rose Will Bloom Again</u>, is my spiritual autobiography. It is filled with testimonies of God's faithfulness, even amidst the most heartbreaking and crushing circumstances known to the human heart.

Clifton's book, <u>Saint or Sinner</u> is a transcribed message that was groundbreaking at the time he first preached it and continues to bless and set people free! This book addresses many of the common misconceptions with 1 John 1:9.

Cody's testimony is recorded. It's a powerful tool for your loved ones to hear who are struggling with addiction.

Another book I've written, entitled <u>Israel and the Church</u>, records my testimony and my experiences from my three trips to Israel. You may order this book or Cody's testimony (we also have CD's and other resources available) from:

Clifton Coulter Ministries
20492 State Route EE
Farmington, MO 63640
(573) 330-8450, 8451

You may reach all of us on Facebook.

My final thought: God has given you dreams, and He has a purpose for your life. Remember, it is never too late to fulfill your destiny. Pray, listen, and move forward! The Lord has your best interest at heart, and desires to bless you even more than you want to be blessed! Trust Him!

Acknowledgements

My first acknowledgment is to the God and Father of the Lord Jesus Christ and to the Holy Spirit. Without Him, I would not be alive to proclaim His goodness!

I owe an ocean of thanksgiving to all who have influenced me over my many years of knowing Him. My husband and children and grandchildren push me on to success, giving me all the support I need, and are my advertisement team!

Andrew Wommack has been mentioned throughout the book, as he has influenced me and trusted in me enough to ask me to teach in his Bible College. My inspiration for this book came from the curriculum I developed while teaching at Charis Bible College.

I wanted to give a special word of thanks to Steve and Susan Prager who believed in me and gave me a two week stay in their Florida beach house to finish this book. Steve has been my friend and editor, ministry associate, and partner with Clifton Coulter Ministries. Being a published author himself, he was able to give me points and advice which has been invaluable in the finished product of <u>Nuggets from the Gold Mine</u>.

Thank you to Empyrion Publishing. Rick and Judi Manis have walked me through publishing my first

183

book, <u>Your Rose Will Bloom Again</u>, and now <u>Nuggets from the God Mine</u>. They, also, are published authors and friends.

And to you the reader: May you be filled to the brim with God's goodness and faithfulness. I pray this book has been an encouragement to you.

Made in the USA
Middletown, DE
06 March 2022